Decorative Painting: Fruit, Vegetables & Berries

Decorative Painting:
Fruit, Vegetables & Berries

Kathy Ritchie

NORTH
LIGHT
BOOKS

Cincinnati, Ohio

A QUARTO BOOK

First published in North America in 1997
by North Light Books, an imprint of
F&W Publications, Inc.,
1507 Dana Avenue, Cincinnati, OH 45207
1-800/289-0963

ISBN 0-89134-796-8

This book was designed
and produced by
Quarto Publishing plc
The Old Brewery
6 Blundell Street
London N7 9BH

Project editors Jane Hurd-Cosgrave,
   Jean Coppendale
Managing editor Sally MacEachern
Senior art editors Catherine Shearman,
   Elizabeth Healey
Designers David Palmer, Jennie Dooge,
   Tania Field
Picture researcher Zoe Holtermann
Indexer Dorothy Frame
Art director Moira Clinch
Assistant art director Penny Cobb
Editorial director Pippa Rubinstein

Typeset by Type Technique, London W1
Manufactured in Singapore by Bright Arts
   (Singapore) Pte Ltd
Printed in Singapore by Star Standard
   Industries (Pte) Ltd

Contents

INTRODUCTION 6

Inspirations 8

STARTING OUT 10

Basic equipment 12
Brushes 14
Simple color theory 16
Color chart 18
Preparing the surface 20
Basic techniques 22
Basecoating 22
Creating different paint effects 23
Brush control 24
Brush loading 25
Tipping, Stippling, Drybrushing,
  Double loading 26
Basic strokes 28
Blending 33
Finishing effects 34
Inspirations 36

FRUIT, VEGETABLES
& BERRIES 40

Round Shapes 40
Inspirations 60
Heart shapes 62
Inspirations 78
Oval shapes 80
Inspirations 92
Elongated ellipse shapes 94
Inspirations 104
Pear shapes 106
Inspirations 116
Additional features 118
Inspirations 122
Index 126
Credits 128

Introduction
Decorative Painting: Fruit, Vegetables & Berries

Since the earliest of times, people have added color to their homes with paint, and the term decorative painting has become an all encompassing phrase which describes painted decoration from simple or folk-art styles to highly developed realistic styles.

This book focuses on painting fruit, vegetables, and berries and aims to simplify some of the many different techniques that can be used to paint them by taking you through step by step. You are offered several alternative styles for painting different subjects either in different color combinations or in a simplified style using stroke work. Sometimes a fun, alternative technique is demonstrated such as spattering your zucchini with a toothbrush (see page 96), stamping a mushroom pattern with a real, cut mushroom (see page 58), or using a cotton swab to paint a blackberry

(see page 64). These techniques can be tried on many other kinds of fruit and vegetables. For example, maybe you could use a cut pepper or chili to stamp out a border or pattern, or you could try spattering the rind of a watermelon. Once you

have tried some of the techniques that are described in this book you will begin to feel more confident about experimenting.

If this is your first attempt at decorative painting you should read the Starting Out section of this book before you begin (see pages 10-35). This section describes the basic equipment, such as brushes and paints, that you will need to start painting. A beginner's kit of materials does not need to be very expensive because some common household items can be used, such as styrofoam meat trays in place of palettes, and ice-cream sticks in place of palette knives.

You may feel a little daunted at the prospect of plunging in and immediately starting to paint. If so, warm up and practice by working through the Basic Strokes section of this book (see pages 28-32).

Mastery of stroke work will give you a strong foundation for decorative painting. Stroke-work borders that incorporate different shapes, such as the comma stroke and the S stroke, are commonly used to add a finishing border to decorative painting. Strokes can be used in many combinations to create the shapes of fruits and vegetables and single strokes and combination strokes (see page 119) are used to create leaves. Remember you can use stroke work on practice paper to help your hand loosen up before you begin to paint.

When you feel more confident about your stroke work, you can move on to try Brush Loading techniques where two colors are loaded onto the brush at the same time (see pages 26-27). Tipping and double loading allow you to create single strokes such as the comma or the crescent stroke which have the colors wet blended upon completion of the stroke. These loading techniques together with blending techniques (see page 33) will open up a new world of

painting for the beginner. Blending allows you to add subtlety in the layering of color in your painting. Once you know how to blend and layer paint you will be able to paint realistic fruit and vegetables.

The choice of what items to paint is endless – old or new, wood or metal. But before you begin to paint all items must be properly prepared. This preparation requires elbow grease, and it is hard and often dull work. However, it really pays off for when you begin the decorative painting you will know that your stroke work will be clean and sharp because you have thoroughly cleaned and prepared the surface.

The motif you choose to paint will probably be dictated by the skills that you develop. Do not be afraid to experiment with many different techniques and color combinations – experimenting will help you to develop your own style. Remember you are not necessarily trying to reproduce exactly what you see in this book. You will have your own way of working and, before long, your own style of painting will develop–never be afraid to try and express it!

Inspirations

Choosing a muted palette as in the painted swan (below) helps to create an antique effect. Alternatively you can choose, as many decorative painters do, to work in the brightest palette and apply antiquing medium over the entire surface afterwards. This has the advantage of allowing you to antique in layers until you have the desired effect.

Ladies on Tray (detail)
Doxie Keller

The pear, grapes, and strawberries were painted using a loose wet-on-wet technique. It has been antiqued, and the antiquing medium has been carefully lifted from the highlighted areas such as the faces, arms, and dresses of the ladies.

Antiqued grapes
Donna White

The grape pattern painted on this swan uses a muted color palette made up of olive green, yellow ocher, and raw sienna to create an antiqued effect.

Country flowers and herbs
Kim Lowe

*The door panels of this country style cupboard have been painted
in a blue latticework design. This is an effective device for breaking
up the large areas of the door panels. You can paint blueberries,
cranberries, or raspberries weaving in and out of the lattice, see
page 118 for instructions on how to paint a lattice basket.*

Starting out

If you are a true beginner at decorative painting, you may not know where to begin when it comes to choosing brushes, paint, color mixing, selecting color schemes, and executing strokes. This section of the book explains all these aspects of decorative painting, together with how to care for your equipment, prepare different types of surfaces, and paint background effects.

Basic equipment

The various types of supplies, brushes, and paints that you will need to begin decorative painting are explained in this section of the book. It is worth noting that you can begin with relatively few supplies and little expense, and that you can add to your collection of brushes and other materials as you go.

Brushes

Brushes are the main tools of the decorative painting trade, the correct tool will enhance your painting, the incorrect tool will discourage you. It is important to use the right brush for the required effect. Choose the best brushes that you can afford and make a wish list of the ones that you would like to buy later and slowly build up your collection. It is worth noting that **synthetic brushes** *are manufactured to simulate the quantities of natural hair at a fraction of the cost. They are durable, easier to clean than natural hair brushes, and come in a range of shapes and sizes. They are highly recommended for decorative painting.*

Beginner's brushes
¼ inch (6 mm) to ⅜ inch (10 mm) flat or shader; no. 4 round; no. 1 liner; 1 inch (25 mm) to 1½ inch (38 mm) flat brush for basecoating.

Note: *The basecoating brush does not need to be an artists's brush, it can be a soft bristled decorating brush.*

Beginner's paints
Napthol red
Ultramarine
Cadmium yellow light
White
Black

Paints

If you are a beginning decorative painter choosing the type of paint to work with may seem confusing.

It is recommended for a beginner to use acrylic paints. They are formulated from an acrylic polymer resin (the binder) which means that when dry, they are water resistant. While wet such as when they are on the end of your paint brush they are water soluble, which means that they can be thinned with water and they can be washed out of brushes with water. Acrylic paints dry within minutes so several layers can be built up quickly and you can see the results of your work quickly.

The **palette** *is the surface onto which you will dispense your paints and mix color. It should be flat and a light shade so that it doesn't confuse you when you are trying to mix different colored paints. Two inexpensive options are to use an old plate or a Styrofoam meat tray.*

The advantage of quick drying acrylics becomes a disadvantage when you want your paints to remain workable for a long time on your palette. Commercially manufactured wet palettes are available from artists's supply and craft stores. They have a reservoir paper which retains water and a membrane paper which goes over the top of the resevoir paper onto which you will mix your paints. They all have tight fitting lids which help to keep water from evaporating and sometimes your paints can remain workable for weeks. They are a good investment if you have become more than just a casual decorative painter.

*A **palette knife** should be used to mix large amounts of paint. When you advance in decorative painting, you can invest in a true artists's palette knife which is either plastic or metal. Beginners can use any flat item that they feel comfortable with such as a butter knife or an ice-cream stick.*

Other equipment

A water jar for rinsing brushes
Paper towels or rags for blotting brushes
Old plates or styrofoam meat trays for palettes
Butter knife or ice-cream stick for a palette knife
Tracing paper for transferring patterns
Soft pencil, artists's charcoal, or chalk
Small pieces of foam rubber for blending and texturing
Toothbrush for spattering or for fly-spotting

Caring for your brushes

Try not to overload your brush with paint up to the ferrule, and do not leave your brushes standing on their heads in water or solvents for long periods because the ends will curl. Try to get into the habit of thoroughly cleaning your brushes not only after a painting session, but also during painting. Brushes that haven't been thoroughly cleaned will develop a knot of paint usually close to the ferrule and become misshapen.

1 The Round *brush comes to a fine point and is used to produce decorative strokes such as the comma stroke, crescent stroke, and the S stroke.*

2 Flats *are divided into two categories. The name "flat" refers to a brush with bristles that are longer than the width of the ferrule. They are used for applying washes and floating color because they can be loaded with more paint.* **Brights** *or* **chisels** *have bristles which are the same length as the width of the ferrule and are used where more control of the brush is needed to produce good, clean, sharp edges.*

3 Filbert *or* **cat's tongue** *is a compromise between a flat and a round brush. It can help you to create very soft edges when blending colors and, because the brush is pointed, you can paint into tight spaces.*

4 Liner, **Rigger**, *or* **Striper** *is a round brush with extra long bristles. It can carry a large load of paint for long, continuous brush strokes and lining work.*

5 Wash mops *are generally used for covering large areas with washes of color and for working wet-on-wet, blending colors together.*

6 Fan *is specifically used for "blending" colors and is often used by water colorists for creating grass and foliage.*

The head *is constructed in various shapes for different kinds of stroke work. It is made up of various natural or synthetic hairs or filaments that are designed to work with different types of paints.*

The ferrule *is the tapered metal tube that holds the bristles to the handle. Look for brushes with seamless ferrules. A seamed ferrule will retain moisture and paint, and will eventually begin to crack and split open and separate from the handle.*

The handle *of a good quality paint brush is usually made of lacquered beech. Handles can be either short or long. Try to choose short-handled brushes, because they are easier to control and you will avoid poking yourself in the eye when you are doing lots of close up painting!*

1.0

M GRUMBACHER N.Y. BEAUX AR

1 *Wipe off any excess paint onto a piece of rag, tissue, or paper towel. Rinse the brush in the appropriate solvent, either water for acrylic-based paint or mineral spirits (white spirit), or turpentine for oil-based paint. Then gently wash the brush in mild soap and warm water.* **Note:** *Do not use hot water because synthetic bristles will become misshapen and natural bristles will dry out. In synthetic haired brushes and in natural bristle brushes hot water will remove the natural oils from the hairs and dry them out.*

2 *A bar of soap by the sink is perfect to draw the bristles of your brush through.*

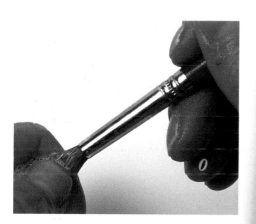

3 *Gently work the soap into the bristles and up to the ferrule. You'll be surprised to see more color coming out even though you thought that you had rinsed it clean.*

4 *Rinse the brush in clean, warm water and repeat Steps 2 and 3 until no trace of paint remains. Then draw the brush through the soap and reshape the head with your fingers. It is best to let the brush dry lying flat, that way no moisture from the head will travel down the ferrule and stay in the handle causing it to swell.*

Note: *You can sometimes reshape synthetic bristles by soaking them in hot, but not boiling water. Then reshape them with your fingers, and allow them to dry naturally.*

Simple color theory

The whole concept of color theory can seem to be intimidating to the beginning decorative painter. Here, you are given an introduction to some of the fundamentals of color theory. You will find that once you understand the color wheel and color relationships, you will confidently move on to color mixing, and that choosing color schemes will become exciting.

The classification of colors

*Red, yellow, and blue are called the three **primary** colors because they cannot be obtained by mixing any other hues.*

*There are three **secondary** hues or colors which can be obtained by mixing equal amounts of two primary colors together. Red and yellow produce orange, red and blue produce purple, and yellow and blue produce green. Orange, purple, and green are the three secondary colors.*

Three hues, yellow, red and blue are more intense on the left than the right.

Red, blue, and yellow are the primaries on this color wheel. Orange, purple, and green are created by mixing equal amounts of the color on each side of it.

The three properties of color:

Hue *is the other word for color. Red, yellow, and blue are the three hues which form the basis of the color wheel.*

Intensity *of a color describes its saturation of color. Colors that are vivid and strong are intense colors. They are saturated; they haven't been grayed by the addition of another color and don't contain a lot of white or black.*

Value *is the lightness or darkness of a color as it relates to the "value scale," white being the lightest and black being the darkest a color can be. The value of a color can be measured independently to its color hue. Other words to describe the value of a color are pale, or pastel, or **tint** which specifically describes a color containing white, and dark or **shade** which is a color containing black.*

Mixing color

The color wheel below shows the addition of intermediary colors. They are produced by mixing each primary color with the secondary color next to it.

Complementary colors are the colors that are directly opposite each other on the color wheel. The complement of red is green, the complement of blue is orange, the complement of yellow is purple. Mixing a color with its complement will make it dull or gray. This can be very useful when you want to "knock a color back" or make it less intense but still want it to remain lively.

Colors can also be deepened in value by the addition of black. Colors produced by adding black are called **shades**. Shades are duller versions of the color and tend to have less vibrancy than colors dulled with their complement because black is less light reflective.

Adding white to a color lightens and it creates a **tint**. Tinted colors are softened by the addition of white.

By mixing equal amounts of two secondary colors you get a third group of hues called **tertiaries** which means "third", not because they are the third grouping but rather meaning that they are produced in various proportions of all three primaries. Orange and purple produce russet, orange and green produce citron, and purple and green produce olive. Russet, citron, and olive are the three tertiaries and if you mix them you will see that they are made up of two parts of one primary and one part of each of the other two.

The same color can look very different when placed against different color backgrounds.

Here each of the three primaries is shown on a light and a dark background.

Different values of yellow and green. The lighter values or tints were produced by adding white; the darker values or shades were produced by addng black.

These colors have been lightened by the addition of white.

+ white

Color Palette

You do not need to copy the colors shown in this book. You can use colors which are a close match or experiment with your own color schemes. The major brands of acrylic paints have huge color ranges. Each range differs slightly in tone and shade. We have used Jo Sonja's Chroma Acrylics but you will be able to find the same or similar colors in any of the other ranges. Although manufacturer's recommend that you do not mix brands, on the whole most acrylics seem to be compatible. When mixing colors, you may find that your mixes vary slightly from the ones in this book, or even from session to session. Experiment with varying quantities of the basic colors until you are happy with the mixed result.

BASIC COLORS

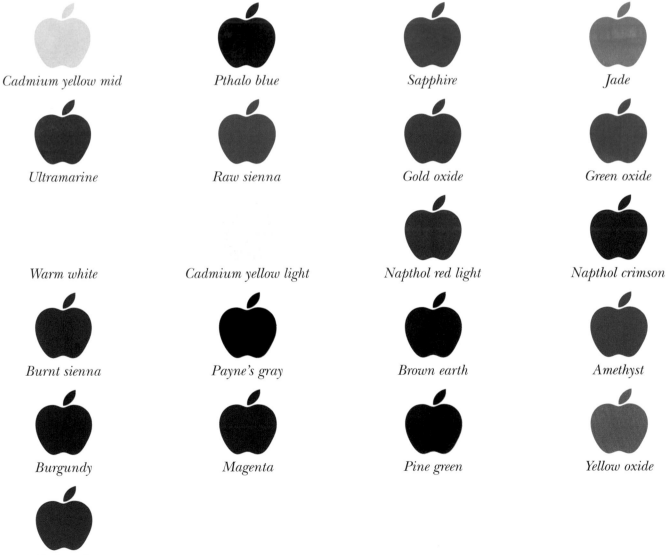

Cadmium yellow mid   *Pthalo blue*   *Sapphire*   *Jade*

Ultramarine   *Raw sienna*   *Gold oxide*   *Green oxide*

Warm white   *Cadmium yellow light*   *Napthol red light*   *Napthol crimson*

Burnt sienna   *Payne's gray*   *Brown earth*   *Amethyst*

Burgundy   *Magenta*   *Pine green*   *Yellow oxide*

Red earth

PROJECT COLORS

SAGE
Green oxide
Cadmium yellow mid
White

PALE PINK
White
Napthol crimson
Green oxide

SLATE
Pthalo blue
Burnt sienna
White

DEEP ORANGE
Cadmium yellow mid
Red earth
Napthol crimson

OLIVE
Pine green
Yellow oxide
Burnt sienna

SUNFLOWER YELLOW
Yellow oxide
Cadmium yellow
White

MAROON
Burgundy
Pthalo blue
Brown earth

APRICOT
Napthol crimson
Cadmium yellow mid
White

SALMON
Red earth
White

MINT
Green oxide
White

SPRING GREEN
Cadmium yellow mid
Pine green

FAWN
Brown earth
White

CREAM
White
Yellow oxide

PRIMROSE
Cadmium yellow light
White

CANARY YELLOW
Cadmium yellow mid
Napthol red light

PALE YELLOW
White
Cadmium yellow mid

DAMASK
Burgundy
Ultramarine

HOT PINK
Napthol crimson
White

SAP GREEN
Pine green
Cadmium yellow mid

PUTTY
Burnt sienna
Brown earth
White
Pine green

PESTO
Green oxide
Yellow oxide

DEEP PURPLE
Burgundy
Pthalo blue

LAVENDER
Ultramarine
Napthol red light
White

Preparing the surface

You will probably want your decorated surface or object to last a lifetime (or longer), and you will also want to enhance the beauty of your painting. To do this, you must prepare your surface properly. This preparation may seem to be tedious and boring, but this can be overcome by setting up a sort of production line and preparing a number of articles at once. This will enable you to move on to the exciting step of decorating objects.

Old wood, *whether it has been waxed, varnished, shellaced, or painted, needs to be free of loose, flaky material and cleaned thoroughly with warm, soapy water.*

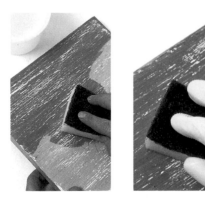

Soda crystals dissolved in hot water according to the manufacturer's instructions are an excellent degreaser, because they do not react with any finish and do not leave any residue. Whatever cleaning agent you use, rinse well with warm water.

Once the wood has been cleaned, it should be examined carefully. If it is painted or varnished, you will need to check whether the surface is cracked, chipped, or crazed. These can be signs that the surface wasn't properly prepared in its previous life. If the surface is in poor condition, then it is best to strip it to the bare wood and start again. There are many commercial strippers available, or you can have the piece dipped in a stripping tank. Once the piece has been stripped, the caustic effect of the stripper needs to be neutralized with a 1:1 solution of vinegar and water.

Paint will not adhere to wood that has a waxed or oiled surface. You will need to use mineral spirit (white spirit) and fine steel wool (wire wool) to dissolve the wax or oil. It may take several applications of spirits and lots of elbow grease. Use soft rags to wipe up the solution, and finish with a wash of soda crystals and water.

If your painted or varnished surface is in good condition, then you may want to consider painting right over the top. The paint or varnish can act as your basecoat. If the surface is very glossy, then you will want to lightly sand the surface with fine-grade (150-grit).

sandpaper to provide a "key" for your paint to stick to. If you don't "key" the surface you may find your brush strokes slipping and sliding across it, which can be frustrating. Don't worry if the surface looks a bit chalky after this sanding – a coat of protective varnish will bring it back to life.

Unfinished or stripped wood *needs to have any dents, holes, or knots filled with wood filler. Fill the flaw so it is slightly higher than the surface. Some fillers may shrink, or the holes or dents may be very deep and will require further filling.*

Once the surface has been completely filled and the filler is totally dry, sand the surface. Working from a relatively coarse grit (80), to a medium grit (120), to a fine grit (150) is a way of letting the grit of the sandpaper do the work for you. The coarse sandpaper will take off the bulk of the filler without clogging. The two finer grits will smooth and level the surface. Sand in the direction of the grain of the wood.

Once the surface is flat, dust it, and if necessary use a very slightly damp cloth to get all the dust off. But make sure the cloth is only slightly damp. Too much water on the surface of the wood will raise the grain, and the surface will develop tiny raised hairs resembling peach fuzz. If this happens, it will have to be sanded again with fine sandpaper.

The surface can then be sealed with a sanding sealer or shellac. Both these products dry quickly, so work in small areas and try to avoid lap marks and runs. If you do have lapping or runs, sand them out with very fine wet-dry sandpaper or very fine steel wool (no. 0000). Your surface is now ready to be painted with an opaque basecoat.

Tinware *items were some of the first to be decoratively painted. There is a longstanding tradition of tin, or tole, painting. Tin items, whether old or new, need to be prepared differently from wooden items.*

Old tin needs to be cleaned and stripped of paint with a commercially available paint stripper. Then if it is rusty, the rust needs to be removed. Use a wire brush, then sandpaper to remove surface rust.

Use commercial rust removers, available from auto-body supply stores, to remove deep-down rust. Wash the tin item in a strong detergent to remove residue from the rust remover, then let it completely dry overnight. You can speed up the drying by using a blow-dryer or placing the tin item in a warm oven. If you use an oven make sure the oven isn't too hot, or the heat may melt any solder that is holding the tin together.

Your tin is now ready to be treated with a rust-inhibitor primer and then basecoated. Spray primers are best applied in several light, misting coats rather than one heavy coat, which will have a tendency to run. Brush-on primers are best applied in several thin coats using a crisscross stroke to avoid lap marks.

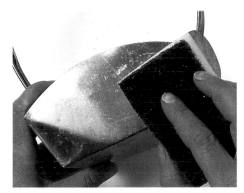

New tin has usually been treated with a thin film of oil, which prevents it from rusting. Wash the item in a strong detergent to remove the oil film. Then wash it again in a 1:1 solution of cider vinegar and water. Let it dry completely and then treat it with a rust-inhibitor primer, and then basecoat.

Basecoating

The basecoat is the first step in decorative painting. It is the paint layer to which your decorative painting will be applied. It can be opaque, masking the surface underneath, or it can be transparent which allows the surface underneath, such as woodgrain, to show through.

which will create a fairly thin, soft glow of color. Stronger mixtures, using more acrylic paint, will create more intense color. You should also remember that the more acrylic you use, the less transparent your "stain" will be. Work in the direction of the grain of the wood, and work in small sections to prevent lapping of the stain. If you want to blend the stain or lift some of it off while it is still wet, you can wipe it with a damp sponge.

▲ Commercially available stains are now manufactured with water bases, which are much healthier, quicker, and easier to use. They are not only made in traditional wood tones such as oak, rosewood, and teak, but are also available in colored tints such as green, blue, and yellow. Always apply the stain according to the manufacturer's instructions, working in the direction of the grain of the wood.

▲ Water-based stains as described above raise the grain of the wood. When untreated the surface roughens. The swelling is microscopic, but you can feel the roughness if you run your hand over the wood. So when the stain is completely dry – overnight is best – you need to sand it with a very fine sandpaper, or buff it with fine steel wool (no. 0000) to take the little nibs off. Then dust it with a cloth and seal it with all-purpose sealer before painting.

▲ Seal your object with all-purpose sealer before you basecoat with opaque paint. For large objects you can use latex paint (emulsion) straight from the can. Give the object two or three coats, depending on the covering qualities of the paint. Sand lightly between coats with fine-grade sandpaper. Generally, it's best to use matte latex if you can. The matte paint levels itself better than semigloss (silk) finishes, and sands better.

For small objects, you can use acrylic straight from the tube or bottle. If the paint is too thick mix it with all-purpose sealer, rather than water for better binding. The more you thin the paint, the more transparent it will become and the more coats it will take to produce an opaque surface.

▲ You can make your own water-based stains using acrylic paint thinned with water in a ratio of 1:8

Creating Different Paint Effects

You will find that your decorative painting will look better, or more exciting, if it is done on some sort of "broken ground." Sponging, dragging, and color washing, are three ways to prepare the surface of your object for later painting. In sponging and dragging, the paint can be applied positively, with a natural sponge or brush, or it can be patterned or lifted off, sometimes called negative application.

In negative application, you need more working time to apply the paint and then to lift it off, so you may want to consider using retarders in your water-based paints to increase the time you have to work with the paint.

1 Sponging

This painting technique uses a damp, natural sponge to produce a patchy, mottled effect. Use paint in a contrasting color; if you want a subtle contrast, tint your basecoat with white. Apply as many layers of color as you like, slowly building the color effect.

Dab the sponge into the paint and wipe the excess off onto a piece of scrap paper. Then dab the surface. Try to turn and change the angle of your sponge so that you produce an even surface. Keep your hand and wrist loose as you work. Try to avoid producing potato prints.

2 Dragging

This is a painting technique in which a brush is pulled across a surface to produce a series of fine lines. You can apply a tinted glaze to a dry basecoat and pattern the paint by drawing or dragging your brush through it.
You can mix a tinted glaze easily by adding some acrylic paint to water-based varnish.

3 Color washing

This technique produces a smooth, softly patterned, subtle finish and can be used in lots of color combinations and built up in many layers. Successful color washing can only be applied over a matte-finish basecoat. Thin latex or acrylic paint with water in a 1:8 ratio to produce a wash. Using a soft-bristle brush, coat the surface randomly by brushing in all directions. A color wash should be protected with a spray sealer, or varnish, before any paint decoration is applied over the top.

Basic techniques

This section begins with an explanation of some of the fundamental techniques such as brush control, paint consistency, and loading. It then shows you how to execute different brush strokes which are at the core of decorative painting. It also provides some valuable hints about how to blend colors either on the brush – for example, double loading, or on the surface – for example, the graduated wash. You will find that with practice your skill and confidence in executing different strokes will grow, and your own individual style will evolve making your painting unique.

Controlling the brush

Good brush control will result in successful brush strokes. The best quality brushes you can afford, kept in the best condition, will help you to achieve successful strokework.

Everyone holds a brush slightly differently, and you will find a way to hold the brush that feels most comfortable for you. Holding the brush upright will give you the best control. For some strokes, such as curving ones, lean the handle of the brush into the stroke to help you make the shape. Try to avoid holding the brush like a pencil, or you won't be able to use the bristles of the brush to achieve clean, definite strokes.

▲ ***Good control.*** *You will need to balance your hand on your little finger and use it like a lever. For some strokes you will find that it is best tucked in, and for some it will feel best sticking out. Your wrist and arm should never rest on the surface that you are painting. You should paint in a relaxed, free-flowing movement from the shoulder, not in a pinched movement from the wrist.*

▲ ***Bad control.*** *Always pull the bristles behind the handle – never push them. If you try to push the bristles, you will find that you won't be able to paint good stroke work. Don't twist the brush (unless twisting is specifically called for) – let the handle lead you into the stroke. Vary the pressure through the stroke, you nearly always finish a stroke by slowing down, easing up on the pressure and lifting off.*

Paint consistency

This varies depending on the stroke you want to make and the brush you want to make it with. Whatever the consistency of the paint, it needs to be well mixed. There should be no lumps and bumps in it, so that you do not end up with blobs of paint falling off your brush in the middle of a stroke.

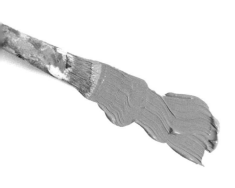

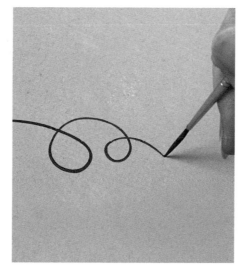

▲ *For long, free-flowing strokes done with a lining brush or a flat shader, your paint will need to be thinned so that you can complete the stroke in one motion.*

▲ *For smaller strokes the paint can be thicker.*

Loading the brush

Full loading *A properly loaded paintbrush will produce complete, beautiful brush strokes.*

2 *Then press and stroke the paintbrush through the puddle of paint several times. Pressing will cause the bristles to splay out, and paint will flow up and between them.*

I *First dip the paintbrush in water to encourage the paint to flow onto and between the bristles. Blot the excess water onto a paper towel.*

3 *Try to load the brush just up to, but not into, the ferrule where paint deposits can build up. Pull flat brushes to a chiseled edge, and twist round the brushes to a point.*

Sideloading *A sideloaded brush has strong color on one side and gradually fades to no color on the other side. You should use a flat shading brush for sideloading, not a bright or chisel, as the bristles are too short to hold enough paint to complete strokes. Dip the brush into water and blot off the excess.*

2 *On a clean area of your palette, stroke the brush back and forth in the same area of about 1 inch (2.5 cm). If you stroke in a bigger area, or keep moving your brush to different areas of your palette, you will unload it and have to repeat the whole process.*

3 *You are trying to move the paint gently across the bristles of the brush, and you may have to wiggle your brush slightly to get the paint to move. You may also have to re-dip the loaded corner of your brush into the paint to get stronger color on one side. You can dip the unloaded side of your brush into water to help the paint flow across the bristles.*

1 *Dip or slide the corner of one side of the brush into the paint.*

Double loading **1** *A double-loaded brush is loaded with two different colors.* **2** *There is one color on each side of the brush.* **3** *The brush stroke will show a gradual merging of the two colors in the center of the stroke. Use a flat brush.*

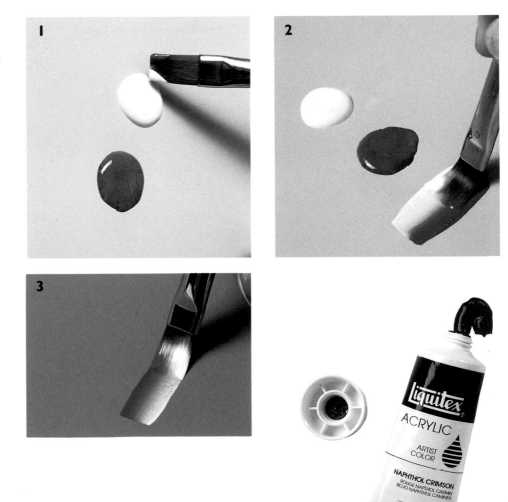

Tipping   Tipping produces a streaky brush stroke by loading the brush with two or more colors. You can use any shape brush for tipping.

1 Lightly load a brush with paint, and then tap it on a paper towel to remove any excess paint from the end.

2 Then dip the tip into the next color. Tap again once or twice on your palette, then complete your stroke.

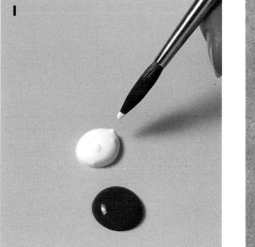

Stippling   Stippling is best done with old, tired brushes or cheap children's brushes that are a bit coarse and stiff.

1 Lightly load a brush with paint and then tap it on your palette to remove any excess.

2 Apply the paint with an up-and-down pouncing motion, or by scrubbing the brush across the surface.

Drybrushing   Drybrushing is a delicate way of adding highlights and texture to your paintwork. Like stippling, it is hard on brushes, so it's best to use old, tired ones or cheapies. Dip your brush into the paint, and work it well up into the bristles. Wipe the paint off onto a paper towel until the brush is nearly dry.

▶ Hold the brush horizontally to the surface and draw it across, barely touching the surface. You may have to draw the brush across the surface a few times to leave a deposit of paint.

Basic strokes

You can use round and flat brushes to create a variety of different strokes and effects. These strokes can be used to build up different shapes, patterns, and motifs. When you are practicing your stroke work remember to relax. Practice your strokes on any type of paper before you start on your object. Keep in mind that you may have to adjust the consistency of the paint to suit the type of surface that you are working on. Save the first practice strokes that you do as they will become a reminder of how far you have progressed.

The comma stroke – using a round or liner brush

The scroll stroke – using a round or liner brush

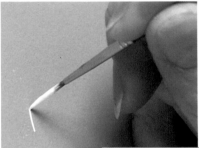

Note: Lining brushes are best for producing long, graceful strokes because they can be loaded with more paint.

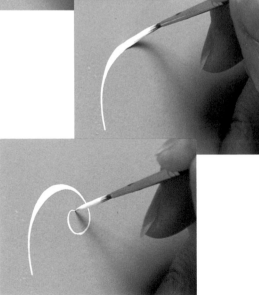

1 Lean the brush handle back in your hand. Begin the stroke by pressing the bristles to flatten them to form the round head.
2 Pull through the stroke in a gentle curve, releasing pressure as you go.
3 Complete the strokes by releasing pressure and lifting off on the tip of the brush.
(See Strawberry page 62.)

1 Begin on the tip of the brush, gently pulling the brush along and following the curve.
2 Apply more pressure while rounding the curve, creating a slightly thicker line. Let the handle of your brush lean into the curve.
3 Release the pressure gradually as you return to the tip of your brush and your and your handle moves upright; lift off cleanly. (See Grapes page 47.)

The S stroke – using a flat brush

Note: This stroke begins and ends on the chisel edge of the brush.

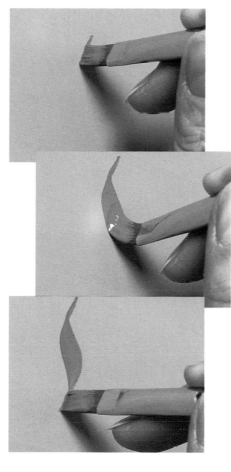

The S stroke – using a round or liner brush

Teardrop stroke – using a round or liner brush

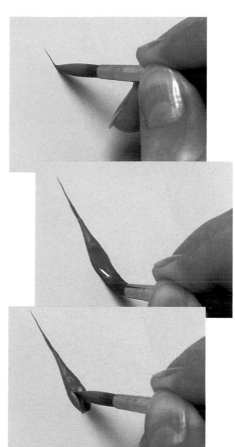

1 *Begin and end with the brush traveling in the same direction. Making sure your bristles come to a point, begin the stroke by lightly drawing the brush across the surface.*
2 *Increase the pressure on the brush on the first curve of the stroke and maintain the pressure as you make the second curve.*
3 *Release the pressure and slow down, allowing the bristles to come to a point; lift off.*
See Additional features page 120.)

1 *Hold the brush upright and begin sliding the brush on the chisel edge.*
2 *Gradually add pressure as you slide into the first curve. Adding pressure automatically changes the direction of the bristles. Then change direction, and begin to release pressure and slow down.*
3 *Finish on the chisel edge and lift off. (See Pea pod page 95.)*

1 *Making sure that your brush is loaded to a sharp point, begin on the tip of the brush, just skimming the surface to form the tail.*
2 *Slide down on the tip gradually applying pressure. Then slow down and pull the stroke to the desired length.*
3 *Come to a complete stop and stand the brush back up on its tip; lift off cleanly.*

**Flat stroke – using a flat
or bright brush**

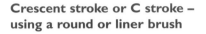

**Crescent stroke or C stroke –
using a round or liner brush**

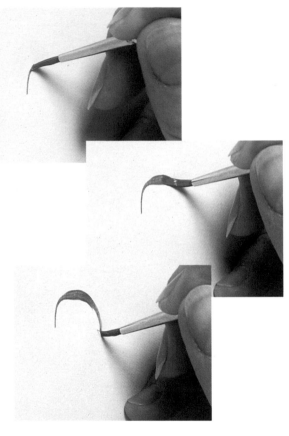

1 *Begin the stroke on the chisel edge
of the brush, using its full width.*
2 *Pull through the stroke, maintaining
even pressure.*
3 *Stand the brush up on the chisel
edge, and lift off for a clean edge.
(See Additional features page 118.)*

1 *Begin the stroke with a fully loaded
brush on its tip. Gradually apply
pressure as you head into the middle
of the crescent.*
2 *Continue to hold the pressure
through the middle of the stroke, and
gradually release pressure as you head
for the end of the stroke.*
3 *Slowly turn the corner of the C,
returning to the tip of your brush
and lifting off cleanly.*

Crescent stroke – using a flat brush

Dipped crescent stroke – using a flat brush

Chocolate-chip stroke – using a liner brush

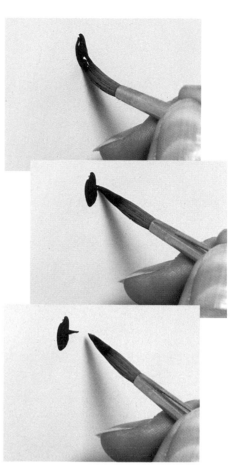

1 *Begin the stroke on the chisel edge, holding the handle upright. Slide the brush along on the chisel edge. Increase the pressure as you pull through the arc of the curve.*
3 *Begin to release pressure as you complete the arc.*
3 *Pull through to the chisel edge and lift off cleanly.*
(See Butternut squash page 110.)

1 *Begin on the chisel edge of the brush, holding the handle upright. Slide the brush along the chisel edge for a short distance.*
2 *Apply pressure as you round the curve. At the center of the arc, release pressure and pull the brush down to create the dip. Then reapply pressure and complete the arc.*
3 *Release pressure and pull through to the chisel edge; lift off cleanly.*
(See Artichoke variation page 76.)

1 *Pick up a blob of paint with the tip of the liner brush. Balance the handle of the brush against your index finger and press the blob onto the surface.*
2 *Stand the brush up, keeping the tips of the bristles in touch with the blob.*
3 *Lightly drag the tip of the brush out of the blob of paint and lift off cleanly. (See Pineapple variation page 84.)*

Circle stroke – using a flat brush

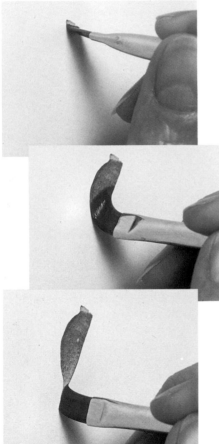

Pivot pull stroke – using a flat brush

1 *Begin on the chisel edge of the brush.*
2 *Apply pressure and rotate the brush through 360° twist.*
3 *Finish off on the chisel edge, and lift off cleanly.*
(See Cherries page 40.)

1 *Begin the stroke using the full width of the brush, with the brush standing on its edge.*
2 *Apply pressure and rotate the brush as you pull through the stroke.*
3 *Stand the brush up on the chisel edge, and lift off for a clean edge.*
(See Pear leaf page 114.)

Blending

Blending using the techniques called glazing, washing, and floating color are all different ways of adding subtle changes in the color or tone of whatever you are painting. You will find that mastering these techniques will add another dimension to your painting. Remember you can use sideloaded or double-loaded brushes to blend your highlights and shadows, and that you can also use drybrushing and sponging to add subtlety to your painting.

Glazing, washing, and floating color

These are all terms for the same technique which refers to applying a trnsparent layer of color over a base-coat. They are techniques that are referred to many times in the step-by-step instructions for painting fruit, vegetables and berries in this book. They are ways of creating shading, adjusting color, and giving something a glow. **Glazing** *refers to paint thinned with glazing or retarder. A* **wash** *refers to paint thinned with water. A* **flat wash** *is evenly colored throughout.* **Floating color** *refers to applying thinned paint over a film of water. In the example below a solid band of yellow color has had a glaze, a wash, and floating color applied to make it a more luminous orangey-yellow color. This gives it more depth than just the flat band of yellow on its own.*

A **graduated wash** *also refers to paint that has been thinned with water. It is a wash in which the color fades from strong to light. Graduated washes are often used when adding shading or highlights to an object. You can apply a graduated wash using the sideloading technique described on page 26.*

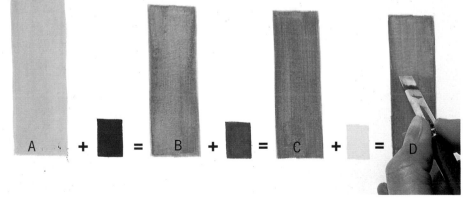

A Solid band of yellow.
B Red mixed with glaze medium and applied to yellow.

C Orange mixed with water and a wash applied to **B**.
D Yellow thinned and mixed with water and floated over **C**.

Sponging with a piece of synthetic sponge can create subtle blending and texture to fruits such as oranges and lemons, and also create highlights. You can use large or tiny pieces of sponge (hold them with a tweezer), whatever is right for the area you are working on. Dip the sponge into the paint and blot the excess off onto a paper towel. Using very little pressure, dab the area that you want to sponge. If you have overdone it, you can always adjust the sponging by sponging some of the basecoat back in.

Finishing Effects

Newly-painted items can stand out harshly against those "aged" by time. You may want to add another layer of texture to your painting and lessen the contrast between old and new by using techniques such as crackle varnishing, flyspotting, and antiquing.

Varnishing

▲ *Water-based varnishes are not as durable as oil-based varnishes so they should not be used on surfaces such as tables, which might receive a lot of wear and tear.*

You must varnish your decorative painting to protect it from wear and tear. Deciding what type of varnish to use can be a bit confusing, because there are so many different types available in at least three different finishes – matte, semigloss, and gloss. You should remember that to truly protect a surface you need to apply at least two or three coats of varnish.

As a general rule, water-based varnishes should only be used on surfaces that have been painted with water-based paints, such as acrylics. There are some new formulations of water-based varnishes available that are recommended for use over oil-based paints. If you choose to use one of these products, you must make sure that the oil-based paints are not only dry to the touch, but cured, or hardened. Water-based varnishes that are painted over oil paint that is not cured can trap vapors that may eventually cause the varnish to peel and blister.

Oil-based varnishes work well over both water- and oil-based paints. They have a slow drying time – six to eight hours – and some are not recoatable for as long as fourteen hours. So building several coats may take many days and lots of patience. Always follow the manufacturer's instructions, as different varnishes do vary. Oil-based varnishes are hard and durable, and are well suited to a variety of surfaces. You need to use mineral spirits (white spirit) to clean them up.

Any varnish you use should be applied in a dust free, warm room. Always apply oil-based varnishes in a well-ventilated room. If they are applied in damp or humid conditions they can trap moisture, which will result in a white bloom appearing under the surface.

▲ *The quick drying time of water-based varnishes is a major advantage when you want to build up many coats in a single day. They appear milky in the can and when they are first brushed on the surface, but they dry clear and can be cleaned up with soap and water.*

Crackle varnishing

In crackle varnishing two varnishes with different drying times are used to create a pattern of fine crazing. Crackle varnish comes in a two-part pack that is available from art and craft stores. Always follow the manufacturer's instructions as they may vary from product to product. A general guide for crackle varnishing is as follows.

Apply the first varnish in a thin, even coat. Let the varnish dry until it is slightly tacky, then quickly brush on a coat of the second varnish with a soft brush, making sure to cover the first varnish entirely. Let dry. You need to be prepared to experiment with crackle varnishing. It is a temperamental finish to apply. Keep in mind that the drying time of the first coat is strongly affected by temperature and humidity and can vary.

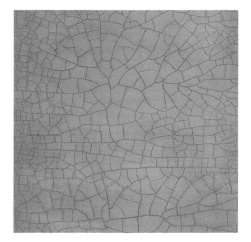

▲ When dry, your cracks may be barely noticeable. You will need to highlight them with artist's oil paints mixed with oil glaze. Earth colors such as brown earth, burnt sienna, and raw sienna are the best colors for an antique effect, but you can experiment with any color. Mix the color with oil glaze and rub it all over the surface with a cloth, a soft brush, or with your fingers.

▲ While the glaze is still wet rub most of it off with a soft cloth, leaving the deposits behind in the cracks.

▲ Let the whole object dry and cure for several days, then varnish it with an oil-based varnish.

Fly-spotting

Fly-spotting, or spattering, can be a subtle way of giving your painting another dimension. You can choose neutral, grayed versions of your basecoat which will tone down your painting, or any of the earth colors, especially brown earth, to imitate fly spots. Fly spots are best applied to flat surfaces; big spots may run on vertical surfaces.

▲ Apply fly spots, or spatter, with a stiff brush, such as a stencil brush or a toothbrush. The paint should be thinned enough to flow freely. Dip your brush into the paint and draw your finger across the bristles – then let the spots fly.

▲ After a minute or two you can dab the spots with a soft cloth (being careful not to drag them), to lift some of the paint and leave tiny rings of color.

Antiquing

Antiquing can enhance your painting by taking away its newness. It can mellow colors and tie them together. However, you need to have a gentle hand when antiquing. There is a fine line between making something look molded and softened, to making it look just dirty.

It is best to give your object a coat or two of varnish before antiquing, so that the antiquing doesn't work itself right into your paint, and so that you have more time to work with it or remove it totally if it doesn't look right.

You can use either oil-based, or acrylic-based artists's paint, mixed with the appropriate glaze medium. Raw umber pigment is a standard for antiquing, but you can experiment with other earth tones, such as burnt umber, raw sienna and burnt sienna.

▶ Mix the paint into the glaze medium, and apply the glaze all over your surface.

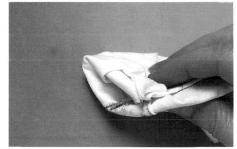

▲ Use soft cloths to lift the glaze from the areas that you want to highlight, and leave the glaze in the areas that you think would be the darkest, maybe in cracks and crevices. Let dry according to the manufacturer's instructions, then varnish for protection.

Inspirations

There are many ways to design a fruit, vegetable and berry composition. You can choose a centered or border motif. You can have a composition that is placed at the top or the bottom of an object, or one that flows over the edges. For instructions on preparing tin surfaces like the reflector on the candle sconce (below) see pages 20 and 21.

Coffee filter box (detail)
Dorothy Whisenhunt
The fruit and leaves are painted to the edges of this octagonal shaped box. The painted water drops on the fruit help the eye move across the composition.

Red plums and Queen Anne cherries
Arlene Beck
The tin reflector of this candle sconce has been painted with the warm tones of Queen Anne cherries and red plums.

The yarn caddy
Linda Wise
This yarn caddy has a marble top and is painted with a bunch of grapes which have very realistic highlights and shadows. The antiquing is deepest around the edges making the grape motif the focal point.

Blackcurrants
Toni Fine (from a design by Deanne Fortnam)
Blackcurrants randomly hanging from a branch have been painted on this letter-rack which has had its sides and rail glazed in green for extra detail.

A pot pourri of fruit with blue birds
Linda Wise
An oval table-top has been divided into eight sections and each has been individually painted with a strawberry, plum, raspberry, red currant, or blue bird motif. A simple line divides the sections and the motifs break the lines to soften the effect.

Fruit bowl on checkerboard
Hugh Logan

The black and white checkerboard pattern in this picture is a traditional folk art motif. The fruit bowl has been loosely blended to give it texture which is repeated in the drybrushing of the fruit inside it.

Cherry trug
Toni Fine

This wooden carry-all has been painted with a corner motif of bright red cherries which stand out against the deep black background.

Fruit and flower swag
Linda Wise
A fruit and flower motif flows over the edges of this wooden lantern-shaped table.

Vegetable drawer piece
Toni Fine
The drawers of this chest-of-drawers have been outlined in a checkerboard pattern and a different vegetable motif has been painted on each of the five drawers.

Still life with fruit (detail)
Dorothy Whisenhunt
Black, green, and red grapes fall over the carefully shaded scalloped edge of the bowl which contains shiny red apples and pears.

ROUND

SHAPES

Many of our most popular fruit

and vegetables are circular in

shape, including all the clusters

such as grapes and vine tomatoes,

which are built up in a series of

round shapes.

Use a simple circle stroke to create small, round shapes such as grapes or cherries and then add highlights and shading to give the shapes some dimension.

Cherries

Cherries are fun to paint, and can be used as a repeat motif around an object or as a border pattern. These advanced cherries with leaves can be used as the focal point of a composition. You can paint a branch with cherries hanging in groups to make a larger composition.

Palette

1. *yellow oxide* 2. *sap green*
3. *brown earth* 4. *white* 5. *burgundy*
6. *napthol crimson*

Strokes/techniques

circle stroke, tipping, comma stroke, drybrushing

Brushes

nos. 10 and ⅛ inch flat, nos. 2 and 8 round, no. 1 liner

1 **Use a no.10 flat brush and napthol crimson to basecoat the cherries using a circle stroke.**

2 Recoat with burgundy mixed with glaze, and use a no.10 flat to repeat the circle stroke.

3 Use brown earth and a no.2 round to shade the "dip" where the stem comes out of the cherry.

4 Mix burgundy with brown earth and, using an ⅛ inch flat, float the color on the undersides of the cherries to shade them.

5 Mix white with napthol crimson and drybrush this pink color to highlight the cherries. Then drybrush over the top using white.

6 Use a no.8 round brush loaded with sap green and tipped with yellow oxide, and build up the large leaf in a series of comma strokes, and the small leaf in two comma strokes.

7 Vein the leaves with a no.1 liner and brown earth mixed with flow medium.

8 Paint the stems using brown earth mixed with flow medium using a no.1 liner.

Apples

Apples are basically red, green, and yellow, but there are subtle color variations. Here you are shown how to paint a realistic apple by wet blending napthol crimson and primrose yellow. You can apply this technique to other color combinations.

Palette

1. primrose yellow 2. cadmium yellow mid 3. napthol crimson 4. pine green 5. burgundy 6. mint green 7. white

Strokes/techniques

wet blending, sponging, drybrushing

Brushes

¼ inch flat, no.10 flat, no.00 round, synthetic sponge

1 Basecoat the apple in primrose yellow, allow to dry. Then paint a layer of retarder over the basecoat. Using a no.10 flat loaded with napthol crimson, paint the top half of the apple. Keep the weight of the color to the left side, and float the color to the right side of the apple. Keeping the bottom edge of the paint wet, go quickly to Step 2.

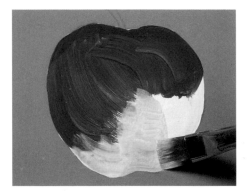

2 Use cadmium yellow mid and complete the apple shape. Go quickly to Step 3 for wet blending.

VARIATION • 1

Simplified green apple

1 Basecoat the apple shape in warm white. Paint two loose crescent shapes in green oxide using a ⅜ inch flat shader. Fill in the center with two more crescent shapes in the same color.

2 Using burnt sienna and a no.6 round brush, paint a comma stroke for the stem of the apple.

3 Use pine green and a no.10 flat brush, and paint an S stroke for the leaf.

3 While still wet, stroke the brush up and down to blend the red and the yellow.

6 Use mint green to paint highlights on the stem and leaf, using a no.00 round brush.

4 Using a ¼ inch flat brush and pine green, basecoat the leaf and stem.

7 Use a little napthol crimson and white to create the highlight color. Drybrush this on and diffuse the edges.

5 Mix the apple shade color using burgundy mixed with glaze. Drybrush the shade color on the left side of the apple and sponge out across the apple to soften.

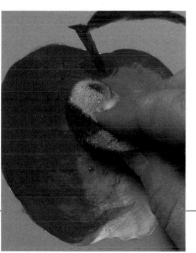

4 *Use pine green and burnt sienna, and paint a big comma stroke on the left of the apple with a no.8 round brush.*

5 *Using white and a no.4 round brush, paint in a big, bright teardrop stroke for the highlight of the apple.*

Cantaloupe

When painting the cantaloupe wedge, it will be more satisfactory if the orange flesh color is mixed with glaze. Use a natural sponge to create the skin texture of a whole cantaloupe, as this would be difficult to create successfully with brush work.

Palette

1. *primrose yellow* 2. *apricot yellow*
3. *deep orange* 4. *spring green*
5. *white* 6. *sap green*

Strokes/techniques

comma stroke, double loading

Brushes

nos.10 and ¼ inch flat, nos.6 and 4 round, no.1 liner

1 Basecoat the fruit in primrose yellow using a no.10 flat brush.

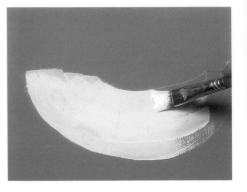

2 Paint over the base color with apricot yellow mixed with glaze using a no.10 flat brush.

3 Mix deep orange with glaze and paint the center section of the fruit using a ¼ inch flat brush.

VARIATION • 1

Whole cantaloupe

1 *Wet blend the cantaloupe shape in white and yellow oxide using a no.10 flat brush. Repeat this step if necessary.*

2 *Use a natural sponge and sponge in cream over the basecoat.*

3 *Mix raw sienna with glaze to shade the bottom of the fruit using a no.10 flat brush.*

4 Double load a no.10 flat brush with spring green and apricot yellow and paint the rind.

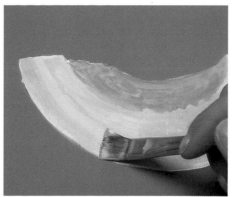

6 Paint a white comma stroke highlight on some of the seeds using a no.4 round brush.

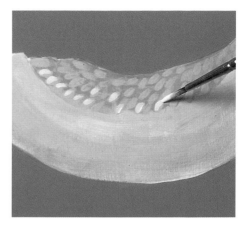

5 Paint the seeds with apricot yellow using a no.6 round brush.

7 Use a no.1 liner and sap green to outline the edge of the rind.

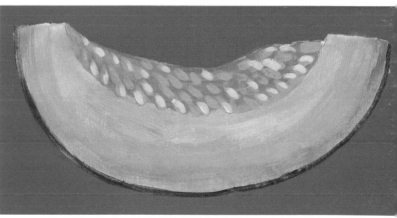

4 *Then use raw sienna and a no.1 liner to line the segments.*

5 *Drybrush a white highlight on the top of the cantaloupe.*

Grapes

Use the same technique to paint both red and green grapes, and vary your palette as shown. If you want to paint black grapes, use the same painting technique and change your palette to include deep purple for the basecoat, and maroon to shade the grapes.

Palette

1. *burgundy* **2.** *maroon* **3.** *napthol crimson* **4.** *raw sienna* **5.** *brown earth* **6.** *sap green* **7.** *cream*

Strokes/techniques

drybrushing, double loading

Brushes

nos.5 and 8 round, nos.1 and 3 liner

1 Paint about 25 per cent of the grapes in burgundy using a no.5 round brush. First paint the grapes in the furthermost background or at the bottom of the bunch.

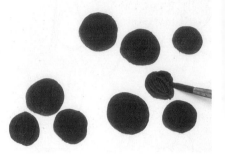

2 Using maroon, paint another 25 per cent of the grapes moving into the foreground of the bunch.

VARIATION • I

Green grapes

1 *Use pesto green for the darkest 25 per cent of the grapes, yellow oxide for the grapes in the midground, and mint green for the foreground.*

2 *Float pesto green over the yellow oxide and mint green grapes to deepen and shade them.*

3 *Drybrush a cream highlight onto the grapes and the stems.*

3 Paint the last 50 per cent of the grapes, using only napthol crimson. By layering the grapes on top of one another, you should begin to see some depth in the bunch.

4 Paint the large stems of the grape bunch with a no.3 liner that has been double loaded with sap green and raw sienna.

5 Shade large stems and add small stems with a no.1 liner loaded with brown earth.

6 Use cream to highlight the grapes. Drybrush the grapes with a no.8 round brush.

VARIATION • 2

Leaves

1 *Basecoat the leaf in sap green thinned with flow medium. Use a no.10 flat and let the brush flutter as you work around the edges of the leaf. Recoat if necessary.*

2 *Using a no.10 flat, float pthalo blue, yellow oxide, and spring green onto the leaf. When dry, use a no.1 round brush to add veins in a dirty green made by mixing sap green and brown earth.*

3 *Hightlight veins in yellow oxide. Use a no.1 liner and sap green mixed with flow medium to paint in the stem and some curly tendrils.*

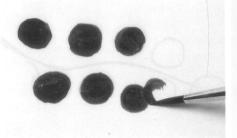
Currants

Red and blackcurrants have a translucent, luminous beauty that can be used to brighten up any fruit composition. Because currants grow in clusters on stems, you can use them to create border motifs, using the stem as the linking element.

Palette

1. *red earth* 2. *olive green*
3. *burgundy* 4. *ultramarine blue*
5. *pine green* 6. *white* 7. *cadmium yellow mid* 8. *burnt sienna*

Strokes/techniques

comma stroke

Brushes

*nos. 4 and 0 round, no. 0 liner,
⅛ inch flat*

1 Use a no. 4 round brush and gold oxide to basecoat the currants.

2 Shade the bottom of each currant in burgundy mixed with glaze.

3 Mix ultramarine blue with a lot of glaze and, using a ⅛ inch flat brush, deepen the shading by painting a single comma stroke at the base of each currant.

VARIATION • I

Blackcurrants

1 *Basecoat the currants in deep purple using a no. 4 round brush. Using a no. 2 round brush, shade the bottom of each currant with a single comma stroke with ultramarine blue mixed with glaze.*

2 *Use lavender to paint a single comma stroke highlight on the top of each currant.*

3 *Use olive green and paint in the stems of the currants. Then with cadmium yellow light mixed with glaze use a no. 0 liner to highlight the stems.*

4 Basecoat the stem with a no.0 liner and olive green. Then shade the stems with pine green mixed with glaze.

7 Use burnt sienna and a no.0 round brush to paint tiny comma stroke buds at the end of each currant.

5 Use white to paint a single comma highlight on each currant.

6 Paint a highlight on the stem with cadmium yellow mid.

4 Use a no.0 liner to shade the stems with pine green mixed with glaze.

5 Use burnt sienna and the no.0 liner to add the tiny bud detail at the end of each currant.

6 Completed cluster.

Cranberry

Cranberries and blueberries are often seen in folk painting native to the eastern region of the United States. The silvery bloom of a blueberry strongly contrasts with the deep red of the cranberry, and they are interesting to paint in clusters in compositions.

Palette

1. *maroon* 2. *gold oxide* 3. *Payne's gray* 4. *white* 5. *pine green*

Strokes/techniques

comma stroke

Brushes

nos.4 and 2 round, nos.1 and 6 liner

1 Using a no.4 round brush, basecoat the cranberries in maroon.

2 Use gold oxide and a no.4 round brush to paint a single comma sroke on the tops of the cranberries.

3 Use a no.2 round brush to shade the bottom of the cranberries in a single stroke of Payne's gray mixed with glaze.

VARIATION • I

Blueberries

1 *Basecoat the berries using a no.6 round brush and pthalo blue.*

2 *Shade the berries with Payne's gray mixed with glaze, using a sideloaded ⅛ inch flat brush.*

3 *Mix white with glaze and use a ⅛ inch flat brush to paint in the bluey blush on top of the berries.*

4 Use white and a no.2 round brush to paint a single comma stroke on top of the gold oxide.

6 Use a no.1 liner and pine green mixed with flow medium to paint the stems of the cranberries and the stem through the leaves.

5 Paint the leaves with pine green. Paint them in pairs, with a single stroke of a no.6 round brush.

7 Use a no.2 round brush to highlight the leaves with white.

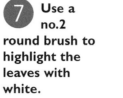

4 *Use white and a no.2 round brush to paint a single comma stroke highlight on each berry.*

5 *With pthalo blue and a no.2 brush, paint the little sepals coming out of the berries.*

Cabbage

Before trying to paint the cabbage as described, take a close look at a real cabbage. With the real cabbage in front of you, read these instructions to see how to develop a realistic cabbage.

Palette

1. *spring green* 2. *sap green*
3. *magenta* 4. *white*

Strokes/techniques

floating color, drybrushing

Brushes

no.10 flat, no.8 round, no.1 liner, no.0 liner

1 Basecoat the cabbage in spring green using a no.10 flat brush. Let the brush flutter around the edges of the leaves. Recoat if necessary. Let dry. Then sketch in the head and the main leaves of the cabbage.

2 Mix sap green with flow medium and float the color to shade the folds of the leaves using a no.8 round brush. Repeat, to give the shading extra depth.

VARIATION • 1

Red cabbage

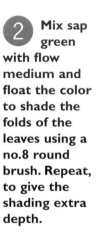

1 Using a no.10 round brush, paint the underside of the cabbage in deep purple.

2 Mix deep purple with glaze and paint the folds and undulations of the cabbage. Begin with the no.10 round brush and step down to the no.3 for the smaller creases.

3 With the no.3 round brush, paint over some of the purple areas with another coat of glaze. Don't try to be too accurate – give an impression only.

3 Use sap green with a touch of magenta to add a purple tinge to the leaves. Use a soft flat brush to blend out the edges.

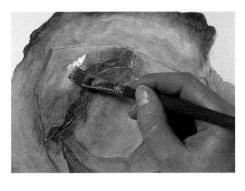

4 Mix white with flow medium and highlight the leaves, using a clean flat brush to feather it out. Drybush some white to brighten the highlights.

5 Use a no.1 liner with white and a touch of spring green to paint broad white veins onto the leaves.

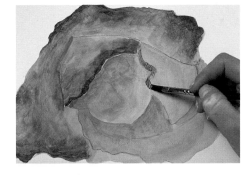

6 Use a no.0 liner with magenta to vein over the head of the cabbage, and add some magenta to the veins of the outer leaves.

7 Use magenta with a touch of sap green to shade in some darker areas.

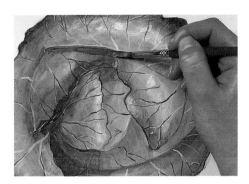

4 *Use warm white to paint the stalk and some of the white areas. Then use warm white mixed with glaze to add some hairpin turns and U-bends over the purple areas.*

5 *Use fawn to tone the stalk where it has been cut.*

Tomatoes

Tomatoes on the vine can be painted as the central image of a design, or integrated within a border pattern, using the vine as the linking element between the tomatoes. Touches of green oxide or sunflower yellow can be used to make some of the tomatoes look as if they are ripening, giving your tomatoes variety.

Palette

1. *primrose yellow* 2. *napthol red*
3. *green oxide* 4. *sunflower yellow*
5. *white* 6. *burnt sienna*
7. *pine green*

Strokes/techniques

drybrushing, floating color

Brushes

⅝ inch flat, no.4 liner, ¼ inch flat, no.4 round

1 Basecoat the tomatoes in primrose yellow, and then paint a second coat in napthol red using a ⅝ inch flat.

2 Paint the stems in green oxide mixed with a little flow medium using a no.4 liner.

3 Shade the tomatoes in burnt sienna using a ¼ inch flat, floating the color over the basecoat.

VARIATION • 1

Simplified red tomato

1 *Paint a background using pthalo blue. Basecoat the tomato in pale yellow using a no.10 flat, keeping the weight of the color on one side of the tomato. Then float napthol crimson over the basecoat.*

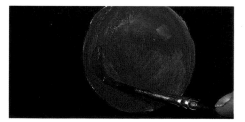

2 *Shade the tomato using a no.6 round brush and burnt sienna mixed with glaze, and paint a comma stroke.*

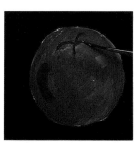

3 *Paint in six sepals, using pine green and a no.1 liner.*

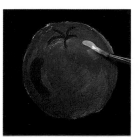

4 *Paint in a comma stroke highlight, using a no.4 round brush loaded with orange.*

4 Use burnt sienna to shade the centers of the tomatoes, where the sepals grow, floating the color.

5 To put in the secondary highlight, drybrush the tomatoes with sunflower yellow. As the light is coming from above, put this secondary highlight loosely in on the top of the tomatoes.

6 To mix the highlight, add a touch of sunflower yellow to white. Drybrush this mix over the yellow highlight of Step 5 to create a crescent shape.

7 Use pine green mixed with flow medium to shade the sepals and stems.

VARIATION • 2

Green tomato

1 *Paint a background in red earth. Basecoat the tomato shape in primrose yellow, then, using a no.10 flat, float green oxide over the tomato.*

2 *Paint the six sepals, using pine green and a no.1 liner brush.*

3 *Paint a highlight by adding a little green oxide to white. Use a no.4 round brush and paint in a comma stroke.*

55

Pumpkin

Warm-orange pumpkins look best when painted against contrasting backgrounds such as blue or deep violet or brown earth. To paint a simplified pumpkin, use a sideloaded brush to create its heart-shaped center.

Palette

1. *apricot yellow* 2. *deep orange*
3. *burnt sienna* 4. *deep purple* 5.
green oxide 6. *white* 7. *mint green*

Strokes/techniques

drybrushing, floating color, sideloading

Brushes

no.10 flat, ⅜ inch and ¼ inch flat, no.1 liner, ⅛ inch flat

1 Basecoat the pumpkin in apricot yellow with a no.10 flat. With a ⅜ inch flat and deep orange, paint the "ribs" of the pumpkin, floating the color with water.

2 Use a sideloaded ¼ inch flat brush and burnt sienna mixed with glaze to float the color over the ribs previously painted.

VARIATION • 1

Simplified pumpkin

1 *Use primrose yellow for the basecoat. Using a 1 inch flat brush, paint two crescent strokes for the body of the pumpkin. Fill in the middle.*

2 *Sideload a no.10 chisel brush with deep orange on one side and water on the other. Paint a heart shape, beginning in the center of the pumpkin.*

3 *Using the same sideloaded brush, paint the rest of the pumpkin's ribs radiating out from the heart.*

76   80   82   84   86   88   90   94   96   98   100   102   106   108   110   112   114

3 Shade the bottom of the pumpkin with deep purple mixed with a lot of glaze.

6 Use a ⅛ inch flat brush and white to drybrush a highlight onto the pumpkin. Drybrush the paint along the tops of the ribs.

4 Basecoat the stem using green oxide.

7 Use mint green and drybrush a highlight onto the stem. If necessary, use another brush to soften this highlight.

5 Use a no.1 liner and the purple shade from Step 3 to line the ribs.

4 Using a ¼ inch flat brush and the same orange glaze used in Steps 2 and 3, paint over the ribs to deepen them.

5 For the stem, paint two S strokes, one over the other, using sap green.

Mushroom

The undersides of mushrooms have a beautiful, deep purple-brown color that can add strong contrast to a painting. Paint simple, button mushrooms with a double-loaded crescent stroke, and you can use mushroom stamps to create a border on any surface.

Palette

1. *gold oxide* **2.** *deep purple* **3.** *fawn*
4. *brown earth* **5.** *pthalo blue* **6.** *white*

Strokes/techniques

drybrushing, lining

Brushes

no.10 flat, nos.8, 2 and 4 round, no.0 liner

1 Use a no.10 flat brush to basecoat the mushroom shape with gold oxide, outlining the stem.

2 Use deep purple mixed with flow medium and a no.8 round brush to paint the gills of the mushroom. Work in loose strokes radiating from the center allowing the outside edge to remain uneven.

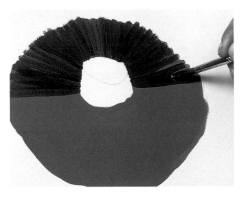

VARIATION • I

Crescent stroke mushroom

1 *Double load a no.10 flat chisel brush with smoked pearl on one side and brown earth on the other. Paint one crescent stroke with the brown earth side of the brush on the outside, or top, of the mushroom.*

2 *Double load the same brush again, and paint the stem, letting your stroke curve outward.*

3 *Add some detail with a mixture of brown earth using a no.2 round brush.*

3 Using a no.2 round brush, shade the stem with fawn and add some detail with brown earth mixed with retarder.

4 Use a no.8 round brush with pthalo blue, with a touch of deep purple, to define and deepen the gills.

5 Use fawn mixed with flow medium and a no.0 liner to highlight the gills.

6 Drybrush white onto the top of the stem.

7 Define the outside edge of the mushroom using a no.4 round brush with fawn.

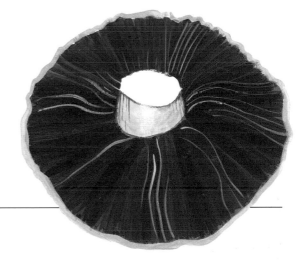

VARIATION • 2

Stamping with a cut mushroom

1 *Paint a color wash in burgundy as explained on page 23.*

2 *Dip your cut mushroom into the paint, or use a brush to apply the paint to the mushroom.*

3 *Stamp firmly onto the dried color wash. Your stamping will have more texture if you do not renew the paint between each stamp.*

Inspirations

If you are a beginning decorative painter you may choose to start painting strawberries that depend on stroke work and have a folk art look such as those painted by Lola Gill (right). Alternatively, there are other styles to try such as those painted by Betty Heron (below) and Tirzah Probasco on page 61 (top right).

Strawberry lamp (detail)
Betty Heron
The tin shade and base of this lamp have been painted in black as a strong contrast to the carefully highlighted and shaded strawberry pattern which curls around its surfaces.

Decorated miniature "Buckby" can
Lola Gill
The design of this can is based on a Russian style and uses a simplified palette and patterns for the strawberries which gives it a folk art look.

Vegetables on antique tin
Nancy L. Genetti
The vegetable pattern made up of radishes, carrots, cloves of garlic, eggplant, and onions has been painted on all the sides of this box. The deep red background color sets off the cool tones of the deep green leaves, the purple of the eggplant, and the warm tones of the carrots and the radishes.

Folk art strawberry box
Tirzah Probasco
The sepal of this strawberry has been painted with broad, green comma strokes some of which have been layered with an additional comma stroke in yellow. The whole piece has been antiqued to give it extra depth.

Hurricane lamp
Arlene Beck
Plums, raspberries, and blueberries in cool shades of dusty mauve, blue, and lilac have been painted around the base of this hurricane lamp.

HEART

SHAPES

Most of the fruits and vegetables

in this section have a dip at the

top and taper at the bottom, so

that when they are reduced to a

simple outline, each resembles a

heart.

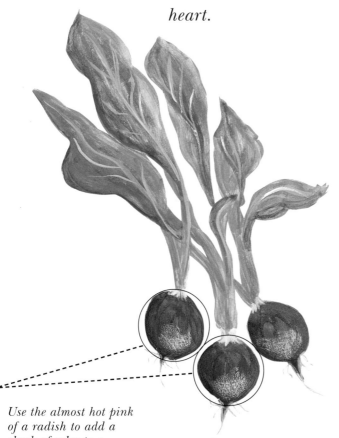

Use the almost hot pink of a radish to add a shock of color to a composition, or if you would like a more muted choice select a mellow maroon coloring.

Strawberry

Strawberries are fun to paint, and work well in patterns because they have leaves and tiny white flowers that brighten a composition. Here, each element of a strawberry, the berry itself, the leaves and the flowers, has been included so that you can see how to paint them.

Palette

1. *napthol crimson* 2. *napthol red light*
3. *brown earth* 4. *cadmium yellow mid*
5. *green oxide* 6. *pine green* 7. *white*

Strokes/techniques

comma stroke, dotting, teardrop stroke, crescent stroke

Brushes

no.5 round, no.0 liner, tooth-picks, nos.2, 4 and 1 round, no.1 liner

1 **Using napthol crimson and a no.5 round, paint four comma strokes for each strawberry to outline the shapes. Then fill in the middle of the fruits with napthol red light.**

2 Paint the tiny seeds using teardrop strokes with a no.0 liner and brown earth. Use a tooth-pick to put dot highlights on the seeds with cadmium yellow mid.

6 Paint the petals of the flowers using a no.2 round brush loaded with white. Paint two teardrop strokes for each petal.

3 Use a no.2 round brush loaded with green oxide, and tipped with cadmium yellow mid, and paint the sepals on the top of the strawberry.

7 Paint a tiny crescent stroke on the outside edge of each petal using a no.1 round brush and cadmium yellow mid, then paint the center of the flowers in the same color.

4 With a no.4 round brush and green oxide, paint comma strokes for the leaves.

5 Use a no.1 liner with pine green mixed with flow medium, to add stems and vines. Draw the lines through to vein the leaves.

Blackberry

Blackberries are easy to paint using a cotton swab to paint the little circles which make up each berry. Use the same technique with color variations to paint raspberries, loganberries and green, unripe fruit.

Palette

1. *lavender* 2. *pine green* 3. *yellow oxide* 4. *ultramarine blue* 5. *deep purple* 6. *white* 7. *brown earth*

Strokes/techniques

stamping or printing with a cotton swab

Brushes

no.5 round, no.1 liner, cotton swab

1 Using a no. 5 round brush, basecoat the berries in lavender.

2 Using a cotton swab, stamp the berries in deep purple.

3 Dip the same cotton swab in white, and highlight the berries with more stamping.

VARIATION • I

Blackberry tipping

1 *Using a no.4 round brush, basecoat the berry shape in lavender. Dampen a cotton swab with water and dip it into deep purple. Start stamping at the bottom of the berry and work up. Allow some of the stamping to bleed off edges.*

2 *Reload the cotton swab with white, and highlight the berry using the same method.*

3 *Load a no.2 round brush with pine green tipped with white, and paint five comma stroke sepals at the top of the berry.*

4 Use pine green to paint the stems. Use brown earth to paint the thorns.

6 Add tiny, white highlights to the berries and then sponge them.

5 Use a no.1 liner to shade the berries with deep purple.

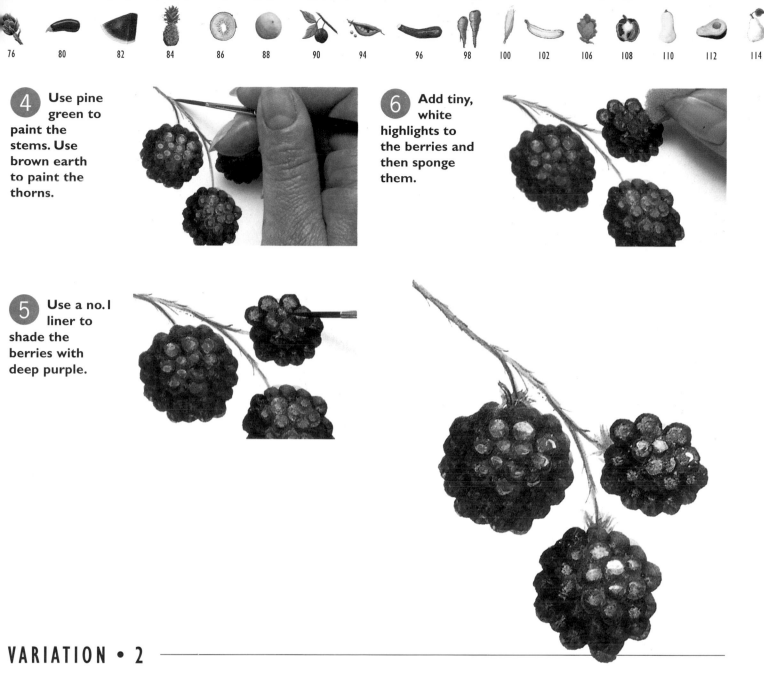

VARIATION • 2

Loganberries, raspberries, and green blackberries

1	**2**	**1**	**2**	**1**	**2**
Base coat	**Stamp**	**Base coat**	**Stamp**	**Base coat**	**Stamp**
Loganberries:	*Loganberries:*	*Raspberries:*	*Raspberries:*	*Unripe berries:*	*Unripe berries:*
Amethyst	*Maroon*	*Pale pink*	*Damask*	*Mint green*	*Sap green*

Nectarines
peaches and apricots

Nectarines, peaches, and apricots all use the same technique of softly blending paint with a synthetic sponge. Getting the subtle color variations between them is the key to painting each so it will be distinct from the others.

Palette

1. *sunflower yellow* 2. *napthol crimson*
3. *white* 4. *brown earth*
5. *green oxide* 6. *mint green*

Strokes/techniques

sponging, tipping

Brushes

⅛ inch flat, no.1 liner, mop brush, no.4 round, synthetic sponge

1 **Basecoat the nectarine in sunflower yellow. Then tone the fruit with napthol crimson mixed with retarder.** The retarder gives you lots of time to work with the paint. Apply the paint/retarder mixture to the top half of the nectarine, and sponge it off to give it texture.

2 **When the nectarine is dry, apply the paint/retarder mix to either side of the crease, using a ⅛ inch flat brush. The paint should be streaky, which will give the nectarine a red blush.**

VARIATION • I

Peach

I *Basecoat the peach in sunflower yellow. Mix apricot yellow with retarder and use a ¼ inch flat brush to paint along the crease. Then use a synthetic sponge to apply a blush to the peach.*

2 *Use cream, and sponge the peach all over to give it a fuzzy look.*

3 *Sponge more apricot yellow or sunflower yellow into the peach to give it the look you want.*

3 To emphasize the crease, paint along it with napthol crimson mixed with glaze, using a no.1 liner.

4 Use a synthetic sponge and sunflower yellow and/or the napthol crimson/retarder mix of Step 2, to tone and blend the nectarine.

5 Streak a highlight across the nectarine, using a mop brush and white mixed with glaze.

6 Basecoat the leaf using a no.4 round brush loaded with green oxide. Then detail the leaf, using a no.4 round brush loaded with green oxide and tipped with white.

7 Basecoat the stem in green oxide. Shade the leaf with brown earth and highlight it in mint green.

VARIATION • 2

Apricot

1 *Basecoat the apricot in sunflower yellow. Then mix apricot yellow with retarder, and paint the upper part of the fruit using a no.8 round brush.*

2 *Use a no.1 liner and apricot yellow to paint in the crease.*

3 *Sponge the apricot with cream to soften and tone it.*

Pomegranate

The pomegranate is a symbol of fertility, and was traditionally painted on dower or blanket chests. Here, you have the choice of a realistic, whole pomegranate that you can paint in combination with wheat sheaves (another symbol of fertility), or a stylized folk-art variation.

Palette

1. **yellow oxide** 2. **white** 3. **red earth** 4. **raw sienna**

Strokes/techniques

comma stroke, sponge blending, drybrushing, wet blending, stippling

Brushes

¼ inch flat, no.3 round, synthetic sponge

1 Using a ¼ inch flat brush, basecoat the pomegranate in yellow oxide. Create contours by blending white into the wet basecoat on highlighted areas.

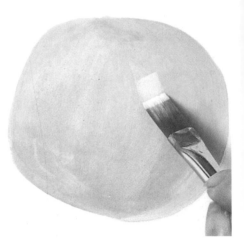

2 Shade the pomegranate with red earth mixed with glaze. Apply the paint with a ¼ inch flat brush, and sponge while wet to add texture. Also drybrush some areas.

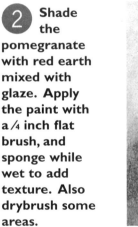

VARIATION • 1

Stylized cut-open pomegranate

1 *Using a ⅜ inch flat brush, basecoat the circle in burgundy.*

2 *Using a no.2 liner, outline the circle with cadmium yellow mid.*

3 *Use cadmium yellow mid to create the topknot of the pomegranate with S strokes.*

3 Using a no.3 round brush loaded with yellow oxide, paint the "crown" at the top of the pomegranate in comma strokes.

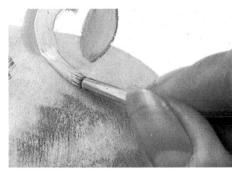

4 Add the shadow of the crown on the surface of the fruit with raw sienna. Then sponge to add some texture.

5 Shade the crown with raw sienna.

6 Use a synthetic sponge to stipple on a white highlight.

4 Use a no.1 liner with yellow oxide to paint "vinework" on the surface of the pomegranate.

5 Use a no.3 round brush double loaded with yellow oxide and white to paint the seeds in double S strokes. Then use white to paint highlights on some of the seeds.

6 Use a no.2 round brush and burgundy to vein the topknot.

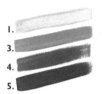

Onions

A key to painting onions successfully, whether they are a bunch of scallions or a single bulb, is to paint fine lines on the bulbs, working around the shapes to create the veining that makes the bulbs so distinct.

Palette

1. *mint green* 2. *white* 3. *yellow oxide*
4. *sap green* 5. *brown earth*

Strokes/techniques

floating color, lining, drybrushing, highlights

Brushes

¼ inch flat, no.1 liner, no.5 round

1 Use a ¼ inch flat brush and mint green to base-coat the scallions. Paint the whole shape including the "greens" at the top. Recoat twice if you are working on a dark background.

2 Float white over the bulbs to brighten them. Then using a no.1 liner and sap green mixed with flow medium, paint fine lines over the bulbs.

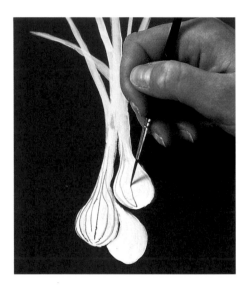

VARIATION • I

Onion bulb

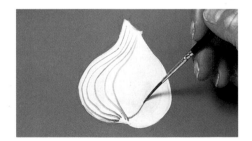

1 Basecoat the onion bulb in primrose yellow using a no.10 flat brush. Recoat if necessary. Let dry. Using a no.1 liner, and burnt sienna mixed with flow medium, draw veins over the bulb.

2 Using a sideloaded ¼ inch flat brush, float pine green mixed with glaze over the lower part of the bulb.

3 Using a ¼ inch flat brush, and burnt sienna mixed with glaze, paint the upper part of the bulb to simulate the warm tones of the onion skin.

3 Using a no.5 round brush, float sap green over the "greens." Then tone the "greens" by floating yellow oxide as a highlight, and then by floating brown earth as a shade color.

5 Drybrush white highlights onto the bulbs and leaves.

6 With a no.1 liner, paint roots on the bulbs using brown earth mixed with flow medium. Highlight the roots with yellow oxide.

4 Float sap green over the underside and around the bulbs, using a no.5 round brush.

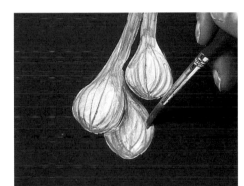

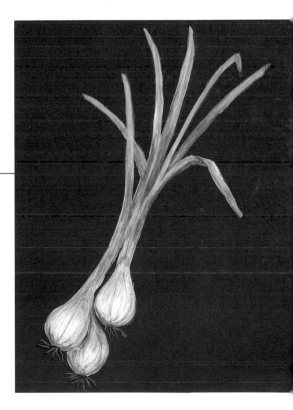

4 Strengthen the veining over the bulb. Using a no.1 liner, paint root hairs with brown earth.

5 Drybrush a secondary highlight of primrose yellow, and then drybrush white over the top.

Radish

Radishes are almost electric pink, and are fun to paint in bunches with their lush leaves flopping behind them. Here are instructions for painting both a realistic and a simplified radish. This technique works well with other types of fruits and vegetables, so you should feel able to experiment.

Palette

1. *hot pink* 2. *burgundy* 3. *fawn*
4. *white* 5. *deep purple* 6. *forest green*
7. *spring green* 8. *sap green* 9. *mint green*

Strokes/techniques

wet blending, lining, drybrushing

Brushes

¼ inch flat, no.0 liner, nos.5 and 2 round

1 Basecoat the radishes with hot pink using a ¼ inch flat brush. Let dry. Paint burgundy mixed with glaze over the top. Basecoat the leaves with mint green.

2 Using a no.0 liner, paint the root hairs in hot pink. Then highlight them in white using the same brush.

VARIATION • 1

Simplified radish

2 *Paint in the leaves using a ¼ inch flat and sap green. Let the brush flutter loosely around the edges of the leaves.*

1 *Basecoat the radish and leaves in warm white using a no.10 flat. Then use burgundy mixed with glaze and paint two overlapping crescent strokes. Then fill in the center, turn the brush to its chiseled edge and taper to the root.*

3 *Ink in the radish with a black lining pen. Loosely follow the outline of the radish, using the pen to add the veins in the leaves and the hairs to the root of the radish.*

3 Use a no.5 round brush and deep purple mixed with glaze to shade the radishes.

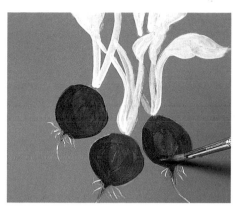

7 Paint the veins in the leaves using a no.0 liner and mint green.

4 Using fawn and a no.2 round paint the stamens at the top of the radishes.

8 Use hot pink to drybrush the highlight in the center of each radish. Work the paint off the loaded brush onto a paper towel so that the brush is as dry as possible.

5 Use spring green mixed with glaze to paint the stems and the leaves. Let dry.

6 Use a no.5 round brush and wet blend between sap green and forest green.

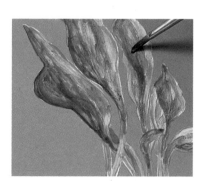

Beets

Beets are similar to radishes in shape, but much mellower in coloring, unless sliced open, when a shock of crimson and maroon meets the eye. Don't be afraid to paint a whole beet in combination with a sliced one, as the contrast in coloring can be very interesting.

Palette

1. *transmagenta* 2. *maroon* 3. *fawn* 4. *sap green* 5. *brown earth* 6. *pine green*

Strokes/techniques

sponging, double loading

Brushes

¼ inch flat, no.4 liner, no.10 flat, no.2 round, no.0 liner, synthetic sponge

1 Basecoat the beets in maroon mixed with glaze using a ¼ inch flat. Paint in the "mouse tails" at the end of each beet with a no.0 liner.

2 Using a no.4 liner and sap green mixed with glaze, paint in the stems. Start at the bottom where the stems begin and build up layers of color to the tops of the leaves.

VARIATION • I

Sliced beet

1 *Load a no.8 round brush with sap green and then tip it with maroon. Both colors should be mixed with glaze. Pull the brush upward, and paint a single brush stroke for each stem. Make a clean stop and lift off.*

2 *To paint the rings on a cut beet, load a no.8 round brush with napthol crimson thinned with glaze and then tip with maroon. Paint in semicircles, working from the outside of the beet toward the center.*

3 *Use fawn and a ¼ inch flat brush to paint the outside skin of the beet. This shape should echo the shape of the main beet.*

3 Mix sap green and magenta with glaze and double load them on a no.10 flat brush. Follow the outside edges of the leaves and then fill in the centers. Build up the color by repeating this step several times.

6 Using a no.2 round brush and pine green, deepen and tone the stalks.

4 Using a synthetic sponge apply fawn to the beets, particularly where the beets join the stems and sides. Use a small piece of sponge and blot it onto a paper towel.

7 With a no.0 liner paint the small roots and hairs. Shade some hairs with brown earth.

5 Load a no.2 round brush with trans magenta and vein the leaves.

4 *Use a no.1 liner brush loaded with maroon and outline the edge of the beet.*

5 *Use burgundy mixed with glaze to add some deeper tones over the main body of the beet.*

6 *Add some white to the fawn color of Step 3 and tone the bottom edge of the beet's skin.*

Artichoke

Artichokes look almost like flowers when painted realistically. Sometimes they are used in arrangements when they are more mature, with large purple thistles coming out of their centers. The simplified artichoke, painted with a progression of dipped crescent strokes, is easy to paint.

Palette

1. *maroon* 2. *deep purple* 3. *spring green* 4. *sage green* 5. *olive green* 6. *white*

Strokes/techniques

drybrushing, crescent stroke, tipping

Brushes

no.10 flat, nos.0 and 4 round, no.0 liner

1 Basecoat the artichoke in sage green using a no.10 flat brush. Then drybrush the leaves with maroon starting at the base of each leaf.

2 Drybrush over the maroon with deep purple.

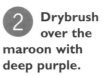

3 Use cadmium yellow mid and spring green mixed with glaze and a no. 4 round brush to make dipped crescent strokes at the top of each leaf at the center of the artichoke. Then use spring green to tip the outer leaves.

VARIATION • 1

Simplified artichoke

1 *Use sap green mixed with glaze, and a 1 inch flat brush to paint the basecoat of the artichoke.*

2 *Mix pine green with glaze, and using a no.10 flat brush, paint two small, dipped crescent strokes at the top of the artichoke.*

3 *Continue painting progressively bigger, dipped crescent strokes. Let the strokes overlap, working your way down until the artichoke is completed.*

4 Use olive green and drybrush from the tops of the leaves down, beginning at the crescent shape.

7 Paint a flash highlight on the tips of the leaves using a no.0 round brush with white.

5 Drybrush a highlight in the tops of the leaves, using sage green.

8 Use deep purple and a no.0 liner, to paint a line on the lower edges of the artichoke.

6 Using a no.0 round brush, with deep purple mixed with glaze, paint some shading on each leaf.

4 *Use a no.8 round brush and pine green to paint three comma strokes at the base of the artichoke.*

5 *Use a no.6 round brush and pine green to paint a pattern made up of three comma strokes.*

6 *Use mint green, and highlight the comma strokes.*

77

Inspirations

Inspiration for painted motifs for different objects can come from a variety of sources such as seed packets as seen on Kim Lowe's Passion fruit wall plaque (right), or on page 79 in Prudy I Vannier's Harvest cupboard. If you want to include lettering in your design, remember that it does not need to be straight or uniform. Notice how the lettering of "Passion Fruit" follows the curved shape of the surface which makes it more interesting.

Fruit bucket
Toni Fine
This wooden bucket has been randomly painted with a variety of fruits such as pineapples, strawberries, plums, cherries, and slices of lemon and apples which add interest. The edge of the bucket has been painted in reflective gold paint.

Passion fruit wall plaque
Kim Lowe
The lettering of this sign board reflects the curved shape of the top and bottom of the board. The deep purple color of the passion fruit has been used on the border to frame the piece.

Blueberry box
Toni Fine
A gracefully arching spray of blueberries has been painted on the lid of this oval box. The edge of the lid has been painted in the same blue color and a scroll stroke and dotting technique were used as a decorative border pattern.

**Harvest
cupboard**
Prudy I. Vannier
*The idea for
painting the
drawers of this
harvest cupboard
was inspired by
three colorful
vegetable seed
packets showing
eggplant, lettuce,
and carrots.*

OVAL

SHAPES

Watermelons and pineapples are

obviously oval in shape, but if you

look carefully at plums or citrus

fruit, you will realize that they are

not round but oval.

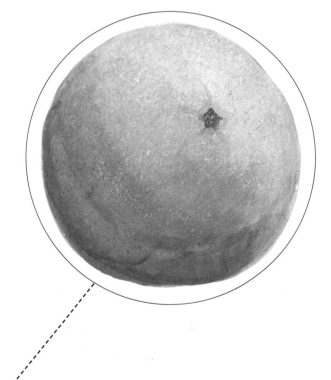

Use the same subtle sponging technique to create the rind texture of an orange, lemon or lime.

Eggplant (aubergine)

The eggplant is a rich, deep purple that is surprisingly simple to paint. It can look spectacular when painted in a composition with other vegetables that have a similar quality of reflective depth, such as tomatoes on the vine.

Palette

1. *damask* **2.** *deep purple* **3.** *spring green* **4.** *burnt sienna* **5.** *white* **6.** *lavender* **7.** *raw sienna*

Strokes/techniques

sponging and blotting

Brushes

no.10 and ¼ inch flat, nos.4 and 8 round

1 **Basecoat the main body body of the eggplant in damask using a flat brush. Paint a second coat with deep purple mixed with glaze using a no.10 flat brush.**

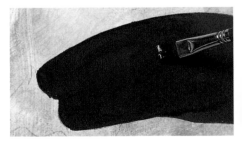

2 Basecoat the stem in raw sienna then overcoat in spring green using a ¼ inch flat brush.

6 Add burnt sienna to spring green, and, using a no.4 round, paint shading and detail in and around the stem.

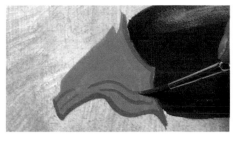

3 Using lavender, paint a reflected light about ¼ inch from the bottom of the eggplant, sponge to diffuse while still wet.

7 Highlight the stem with the spring green mixed with white.

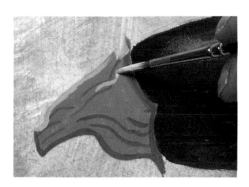

4 Repeat Step 3 about a ¼ inch from the top of the eggplant, sponging to diffuse.

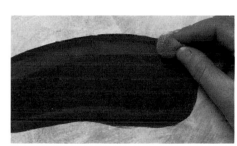

5 Add white to the color used in Steps 3 and 4, and, using a no.8 round brush, paint in the final highlight. While this is still wet, sponge it to diffuse, or blot it using paper towel around the end of a finger, which may give you more control. Also add circular highlights at the bulging end of the eggplant.

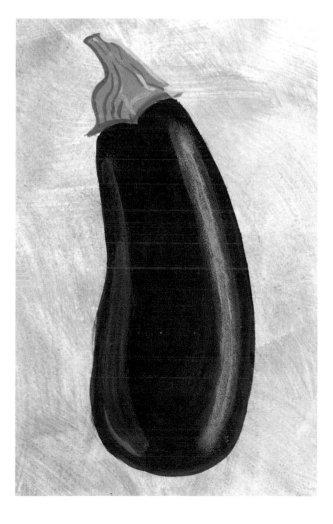

Watermelon

This technique introduces a new twist on marbling for painting a whole watermelon. You can paint watermelons as wedges, using their pink flesh to contrast with the green rind, or as a marblized whole watermelon to decorate something to give a feeling of summertime freshness.

Palette

1. *primrose yellow* 2. *spring green*
3. *napthol crimson* 4. *burgundy*
5. *deep purple* 6. *white*

Strokes/techniques

floating color, stippling

Brushes

¼ inch flat, nos.2 and 8 round, no.2 liner

1 Using a ¼ inch flat brush and primrose yellow, paint the light part of the rind. Use a no.2 liner and spring green to paint the outermost part of rind. Float the spring green into the primrose yellow to create a subtle blending of the two colors.

2 Using a ¼ inch flat brush, basecoat the fruit of the watermelon with napthol crimson mixed with glaze.

VARIATION • I

Seed detail

1 *Paint the shadow of the seeds in burgundy mixed with glaze. Paint side views and whole views of the seeds.*

2 *Paint the seeds in deep purple. Paint them in the areas where you have painted their shadows, allowing some of the shadow color to remain.*

3 *Highlight the seeds by wet blending them with white and deep purple.*

3 Use a no.8 round brush and napthol crimson mixed with glaze to stipple into the areas where seeds are going to be. Add another layer of napthol crimson and glaze to shade the side of the wedge. Use another brush and water to blend out the stippling if necessary.

4 Paint the shadows for the seeds with burgundy mixed with glaze.

5 Paint in the seeds, using a no.2 round brush and deep purple.

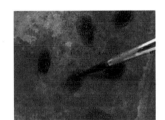

6 Highlight the seeds with white mixed with glaze. Brighten the highlight with a single, white stroke on some of the seeds. Deepen the shading on the side of the wedge with another layer of napthol crimson and glaze.

VARIATION • 2

Whole watermelon

1 *Basecoat the watermelon in green oxide using a no.10 flat brush. Recoat if necessary.*

2 *Use a natural sponge with mint green and sponge in the color variation on the rind.*

3 *Use the sponge with white to emphasize the variation. Then sponge the base color into it to soften the lines. Use a no.2 round brush with raw sienna to paint the dip of the stem.*

Pineapple

The pineapple is a symbol of hospitality or welcome, and is often seen in carved moldings over entrances of houses or as a feature in dining rooms. You can paint it as the crowning focal point in the centerpiece of a fruit composition, either in a realistic or folk-art style.

Palette

1. *sunflower yellow* 2. *brown earth*
3. *burnt sienna* 4. *green oxide*

Strokes/techniques

chocolate-chip stroke, drybrushing

Brushes

no.10 and ¼ inch flat, nos.1 and 4 liner, no.4 round

1 Basecoat the pineapple in sunflower yellow, using a no.10 flat brush. Then, with a no.4 liner and the base color, paint some chocolate-chip strokes to create the spiky outline of the fruit.

2 Use a no.1 liner and brown earth to paint the diamond shapes across the surface of the pineapple.

3 Using a no.10 flat, drybrush burnt sienna into the diamond shapes. Build up the drybrushing in layers.

VARIATION • I

Folk-art pineapple

1 *Using a ¼ inch flat brush, basecoat the pineapple in red earth.*

2 *Build the diamond shapes with brown earth comma strokes. Use nos.2 and 4 lining brushes to give the comma strokes different weights.*

3 *Use a ¼ inch flat brush and basecoat the leaves in pesto green.*

4 Use a no.4 liner with brown earth to paint chocolate-chip stroke spikes in the center of the diamonds.

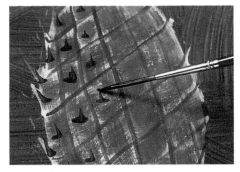

5 Base coat the leaves using a ¼ inch flat brush with green oxide.

6 Shade the leaves in brown earth mixed with glaze, using a no.4 round. Highlight the leaves using sunflower yellow. Drybrush another highlight layer over the top.

4 *Using a no.4 liner loaded with burnt sienna and tipped with white, paint chocolate-chip strokes in the center of the diamonds.*

5 *Using a no.4 liner, highlight the leaves by loading the brush with yellow oxide tipped with white. Paint a fan of comma strokes in the center of the leaves, tipping the liner as you did in the leaf highlight.*

Kiwi

The kiwi is an exotic fruit that looks best when painted as a slice because of its unusual green color and light radiating out of its center. You might want to use it in compositions that include other fruits, such as a watermelon (sliced or whole), or citrus fruits, such as oranges, lemons, and limes.

Palette

1.
2.
3.
4.

1. *mint green* 2. *sap green* 3. *spring green* 4. *brown earth*

Strokes/techniques

floating color

Brushes

no.10 and ⅛ inch flat, no.0 liner

1 Basecoat the kiwi in mint green, using a no.10 flat brush. Then create the center shape, and outline the kiwi using sap green mixed with glaze, and float the color with a ⅛ inch flat brush.

2 Use spring green mixed with glaze to float another layer of color away from the center shape.

VARIATION • I

Whole kiwi

1 Paint a basecoat on the kiwi in putty green, using a no.10 flat brush. Then use a synthetic sponge to sponge in a highlight with white.

2 Sponge in a shadow color, using olive green.

3 Sponge over the whole kiwi with putty green and then fawn.

3 Use mint green and a no.0 liner to paint in the veins radiating out from the center.

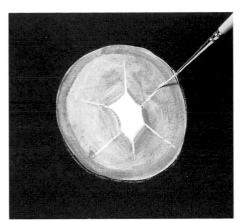

5 Paint the seeds between the veins, using brown earth and the no.0 liner.

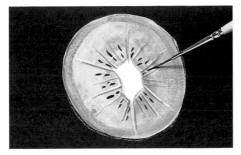

4 Using the no.0 liner brush, shade the veins with sap green.

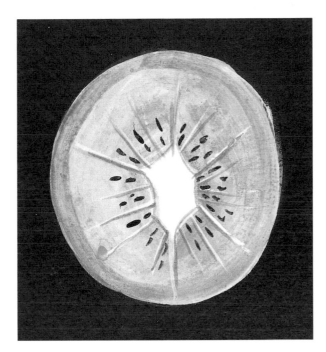

4 *Outline the kiwi, painting in the "knobby" detail at each end, using a no.0 liner and brown earth.*

5 *Complete fuzzy kiwi fruit.*

 # Citrus fruits

Painting oranges, lemons, and limes involves using the same technique with a synthetic sponge to create the rind texture. You can choose one to paint to create a fruit composition, or use all of them to highlight the strikingly different colors of each.

Palette

1. *apricot yellow* 2. *deep orange*
3. *sunflower yellow* 4. *white* 5. *green oxide*

Strokes/techniques

floating color, sponging, sideloading

Brushes

no. 8 round, ⅜ inch flat, synthetic sponge

1 Basecoat the orange in apricot yellow. Let dry. Then shade using deep orange mixed with glaze. Using a no. 8 round, float the color out to get a really soft blending.

2 Add another layer of shading using deep orange mixed with glaze. This time use a ⅜ inch flat brush to float the color.

VARIATION • 1

Lemon

1 *Basecoat the lemon in cadmium yellow. Shade the bottom of the fruit in raw sienna mixed with glaze using a sideloaded ⅜ inch flat brush.*

2 *Paint in the stem of the lemon with sap green. Sponge on a white highlight.*

3 *The completed lemon.*

3 Paint in a secondary highlight using sunflower yellow mixed with glaze. Use a no. 8 round brush and float the color.

5 Use green oxide to paint in the little green "stem" of the orange.

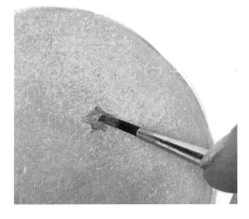

4 Use a synthetic sponge to sponge on a highlight with white.

VARIATION • 2

Lime

1 *Basecoat the lime in spring green. Shade with brown earth mixed with glaze. Use a no.8 round brush to float the color.*

2 *Use a synthetic sponge to apply a secondary highlight of cadmium yellow mid.*

3 *Sponge in the highlight on the lime in primrose yellow. Then sponge the lime with spring green to adjust the toning, and to give it texture.*

Plum

Plums provide a lot of flexibility of color choice – red, green, or purple – to suit your particular composition. You should be comfortable substituting the palette of one style shown here with another if you choose to paint a more simplified or complex plum in a different color.

Palette

1. *brown earth* 2. *pesto green*
3. *burgundy* 4. *deep purple* 5. *hot pink*
6. *yellow oxide* 7. *pine green*

Strokes/techniques

stippling, drybrushing

Brushes

¼ inch flat, nos.0 and 1 liner

1 Use a ¼ inch flat brush and basecoat the plum in burgundy. Basecoat the leaves in pesto green and the twig in brown earth.

2 To shade the plum, stipple it in deep purple using an old brush. Use a no.1 liner and deep purple to paint the crease in the plum.

3 Highlight the plum by stippling it with hot pink.

VARIATION • I

Green plum

2 *Add a drybrushed white highlight to the plum and stalk.*

1 *Basecoat the plum with pesto green, using a no.10 flat brush. Use brown earth for the stalk using a no.2 round.*

3 *Shade the plum and paint in the crease with pine green, using a no.1 liner.*

4 *Soften the highlight by drybrushing again with pesto green.*

4 Drybrush a highlight onto the leaves and twig, using yellow oxide.

6 Use a no.0 liner and brown earth, and shade the veins and stems. Add another line to the bottom edge of each leaf in brown earth. Drybrush over the veins with pesto green to soften them.

5 Use a no.1 liner loaded with pine green mixed with glaze and paint in the veins and stems of the leaves. Add an outline to the bottom edge of each leaf in pine green.

VARIATION • 2

Purple plum

1 *If you are working on a light-colored background, use a ⅜ inch flat brush to basecoat the plum in deep purple. While the basecoat is still wet, rinse the brush and use it to lift out the color, creating a crease and contours.*

2 *Using a no 2 liner and brown earth, add the stalk and deepen the shade of the crease.*

3 *Drybrush the highlight onto the plum with white.*

Inspirations

When you are looking at objects and deciding how to paint them always think carefully about all the surfaces both inside and out. Clayre Sanders's tin cup (below left) was painted on the rim, and Nancy L. Genetti's wooden box (right) was painted around the base. In both cases the objects look more finished when all surfaces have been considered.

Strawberries with flowers on tin
Clayre Sanders
The strawberry pattern on this tin cup was used both on the outside and the rim giving it a uniform appearance.

Fresh vegetables (detail)
Nancy L. Genetti
A cauliflower was used as the focal point of this vegetable pattern which includes asparagus, artichokes, potatoes, eggplant, and squash. Dark green and white leaves, and branches of wheat are painted out from the center of the pattern. The dark green leaf pattern is also painted around the base of the box as a unifying element.

Painted plaque (detail)
Nancy L. Genetti
This plaque includes a simplified watermelon and cantaloupe slice. The light source is coming from the left side – note how the fruits have been painted with a strong highlight on their left.

Banquet fruit (detail)
Arlene Beck
Watermelon, pears, plums, apples, and grapes are used to create a banquet of fruit on this serving tray.

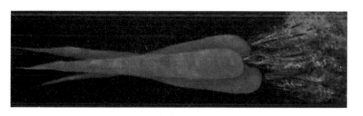

Vegetables on table leaf (detail)
Nancy L. Genetti
A vividly painted bunch of carrots decorates the drop-leaf of a black-painted table. The corners of the table top are adorned with other vegetables.

ELONGATED ELIPSE

SHAPES

Apparently straight fruit and

vegetables such as zucchini or

bananas are, in fact, eliptical shapes

with slightly curved profiles.

Use eliptical shapes such as bananas to break up a painting and add focus to a composition by helping the viewer's eye to move through it.

Pea pod with peas

You can teach yourself to paint peas by beginning with the steps for painting a single pea, then painting a pea pod. You will then be able to progress easily to combining the two by painting an open pod with peas spilling out.

Palette

1. *mint green* 2. *sap green* 3. *pine green* 4. *spring green* 5. *burnt sienna* 6. *cadmium yellow mid*

Strokes/techniques

S stroke, comma stroke, drybrushing

Brushes

no.10 and ⅛ inch flat, no.5 filbert, no.4 round, nos.0 and 1 liner

1 **Basecoat the pea pod, and the detail at the top of the pod, in mint green using a no.10 flat brush.**

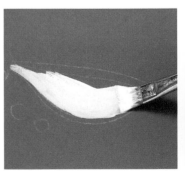

2 Use sap green mixed with glaze, and a no.5 filbert brush to paint an **S** stroke for the bottom half of the pea pod. Let the bottom half of the stroke really drop down to create the open space that will later be filled with peas. Then paint the top half of the pea pod in sap green, using a no.4 round brush.

3 Using sap green and a no.4 round brush, paint the detail at the top of the pod, adding two comma strokes. Paint a tail at the end of the pod, using a no.1 liner.

4 Use a no.0 liner and sap green to outline the shape of the peas.

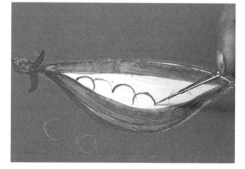

5 Paint the shading inside the pod in two layers, using a ⅛ inch flat brush. The first layer is pine green mixed with glaze, and the second layer is burnt sienna mixed with glaze. Then use burnt sienna and a no.1 liner to paint a fine line along the top edge of the bottom pod.

6 Use a no.4 round brush to wet blend spring green and sap green to paint the peas inside the pod, and the two peas outside.

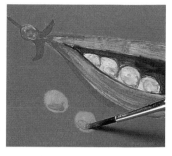

7 Shade both halves of the pod, and the top detail, using a ⅛ inch flat, and pine green mixed with glaze. Add a comma stroke in pine green to the underside of each pea.

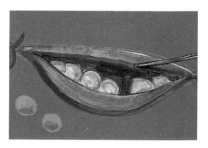

8 Use a ⅛ inch flat brush, and cadmium yellow mid, to drybrush a highlight along the top of the pod, and the top detail. Highlight the peas using the same color and brush.

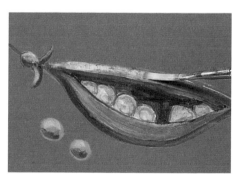

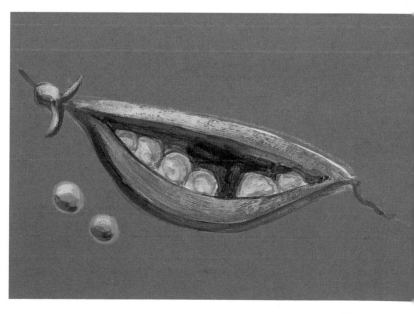

Zucchini (courgette)

The deep green of the zucchini strongly contrasts with the bright yellow-orange of its flower. The flower is proportionally at least as big as the zucchini extending out of it, so it will be a fairly large element in a composition.

Palette

1. pine green 2. sap green 3. cream
4. deep purple 5. mint green

Strokes/techniques

drybrushing, spattering

Brushes

no.2 round, toothbrush

1 Basecoat the zucchini in pine green.

2 Paint the end of the zucchini in cream.

3 Lay tracing paper over the zucchini, and trace the main body (the green part), keeping slightly inside the outer edge. Use a craft knife to cut out the zucchini shape. Lay your tracing paper back over the zucchini, and use masking tape to hold it in place. Spatter the zucchini with cream mixed with flow medium using a toothbrush.

VARIATION • I

Zucchini flower

1 *Basecoat the zucchini flower in cadmium yellow mid.*

2 *Use deep orange mixed with glaze to shade the petals of the flower. Use a no.10 flat brush and float the color.*

3 *Paint the central veins of the petals in the foreground with spring green. Use a sideloaded ⅜ inch flat brush and float the color.*

4 Use a no.2 round brush to paint an outline around the tip of the zucchini, in sap green.

6 Use mint green mixed with glaze and paint a veil of color as a secondary highlight.

5 Shade the bottom of the zucchini with deep purple mixed with glaze. Use a no.2 round brush and deep purple to paint "facet" lines running from the tip of the zucchini.

7 Drybrush a highlight of mint green over the secondary highlight.

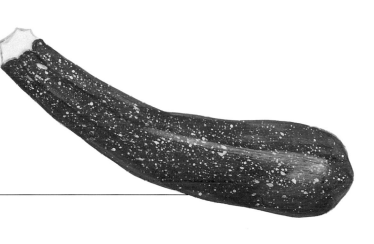

4 *Sideload a ³⁄₈ inch flat brush with white mixed with glaze and paint a highlight on the petals.*

5 *Use a no.0 round brush and spring green to paint small side veins.*

6 *Drybrush more white highlight onto the petals.*

Carrots

Carrots are fun to paint in bunches, and can be used in combination with other root vegetables such as onions and radishes to create an interesting vegetable motif. Paint a border using the comma-stroke carrot variation, painting the carrots end-to-end.

Palette

1. *deep orange* 2. *apricot yellow*
3. *burnt sienna* 4. *brown earth* 5. *pine green* 6. *cadmium yellow mid*

Strokes/techniques

drybrushing, tipping

Brushes

no.10 flat, nos.4 and 5 round. no.1 liner

1 Basecoat the carrot using deep orange, and a no.10 flat brush.

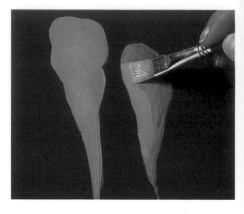

2 Drybrush a secondary highlight on the carrot with apricot yellow

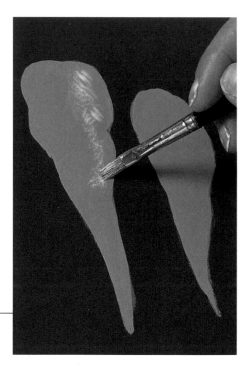

VARIATION • I

Comma-stroke carrot

1 *Use a no.8 round brush, and deep orange, and paint a dipped crescent shape at the top of the carrot. Then paint comma strokes on the left side of the carrot.*

2 *Use a no.8 round brush loaded with cadmium yellow mid, and paint comma strokes on the right side of the carrot. Use deep orange to fill in the center.*

3 *Accent the contours of the carrot with broken lines down the left side, using a black lining pen.*

3 Using a no.5 round brush sideloaded with burnt sienna mixed with glaze, shade one side of the carrots. Draw this shading out horizontally across the carrot to create some contours.

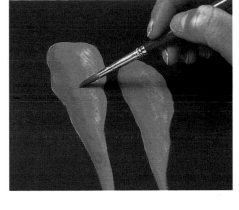

4 Using a no.4 round brush tipped with brown earth and pine green, paint in the pit at the top of the carrot.

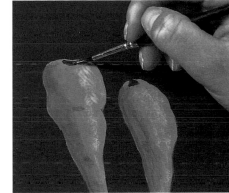

5 Drybrush a highlight with cadmium yellow mid.

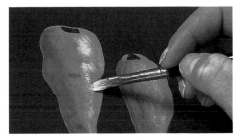

6 Use a no.1 liner and burnt sienna, and loosely paint the root hairs, and lines, running across the carrot.

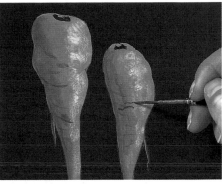

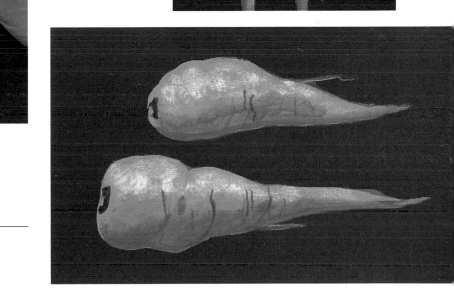

VARIATION • 2

Carrot tops

1 Use a no.4 liner and create the shapes of the stalks using alternately pine green, sap green and spring green.

2 Use a no.4 liner and paint random layers of spring green and sap green to paint the outermost parts of the carrot tops.

3 Using a no.2 round brush, paint teardrop strokes for each tiny leaf in layers of spring green, sap green and pine green.

Corn

Corn, or maize, as it is sometimes called, can be painted singly or in clusters with some of the husk peeling back to reveal the ear of corn inside. As a variation you can paint Thanksgiving corn using warm earth tones such as yellow ocher, burnt sienna, and brown earth.

Palette

1. *primrose yellow* 2. *jade green*
3. *white* 4. *burnt sienna* 5. *mint green*
6. *putty* 7. *cadmium yellow mid*

Strokes/techniques

tipping, floating color

Brushes

¼ inch and ⅜ inch flat, no.0 liner, no.0 round

1 Basecoat the corn in primrose yellow. Base coat the husk and the stem of the corn in jade green.

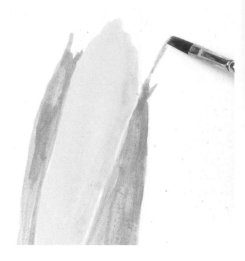

2 Load a ⅜ inch flat brush with jade green tipped in white, and paint over the husk, drawing the stroke up vertically.

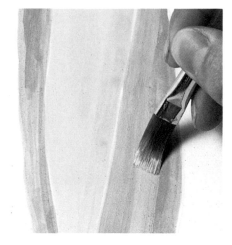

VARIATION • I

Thanksgiving corn

I *Using a ⅜ inch flat brush, basecoat the corncob with a mix of white, cadmium yellow deep and burnt sienna, thinned to a wash.*

2 *Basecoat the husk, using a wash of pine green and burnt sienna. Shade the husk with a wash of the green base mixed with Payne's gray.*

3 *Paint in the kernels of corn, using a ⅛-inch flat brush. Paint each individual kernel in single stroke on the flat of the brush, using burnt sienna, yellow ocher and brown earth, each mixed down with the cob basecoat.*

3 Use burnt sienna mixed with glaze, and a no.0 liner to paint in the shape of the kernels. Work up the corn in vertical rows. Allow the rows to be uneven.

5 Paint cadmium yellow mid kernels on the cob. Using a no.0 round brush, highlight these with white.

7 Paint the fibers at the top of the husk and cob with mint green, using a no.0 liner. Paint the tips of the hairs, using the same liner loaded with burnt sienna.

4 Mix mint green with glaze, and using a ¼ inch flat brush, paint a tissue of husk over the corncob.

6 Shade the husk with putty, using a sideloaded ¼ inch flat brush and floating the color.

4 *Paint comma strokes with a no.0 liner, and "scallop" the kernels to give them some definition. Then paint the fibers at the top, using a no.0 liner and mint green. Paint the tips of the fibers with brown earth.*

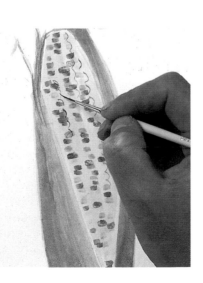

Banana

A banana is a good addition to a fruit composition because it has a curving, elongated shape, which is quite different from other fruits. You can paint them in yellow to add brightness, or in green for something different.

Palette

1. *primrose yellow* 2. *sap green*
3. *cadmium yellow mid* 4. *yellow oxide*
5. *brown earth* 6. *white*

Strokes/techniques

drybrushing, sideloading

Brushes

no.10 and ¼ inch flat, no.4 liner, nos.2 and 8 round.

1 Basecoat the banana in primrose yellow, using a no.10 flat brush. Recoat if necessary.

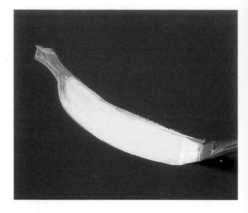

2 Tone the banana with cadmium yellow mid mixed with glaze, using a no.10 flat.

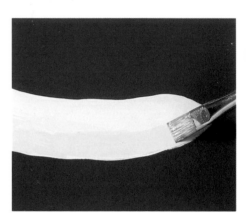

VARIATION • I

Green banana

1 *Double load a ¼ inch flat brush with sap green and spring green, and paint a basecoat following the contours of the banana shape.*

2 *Use spring green mixed with glaze, and tone the complete banana shape, using a no.10 flat brush.*

3 *Highlight the banana with cadmium yellow light, by floating the color along the top, using a ⅛ inch flat brush.*

3 Paint in the facets of the banana, using sap green mixed with glaze, and a no.4 liner.

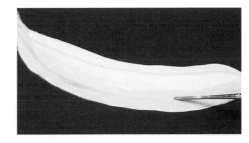

4 Use sap green mixed with glaze, and a no.8 round brush, to add a green tinge to the banana. Deepen the color by adding another layer.

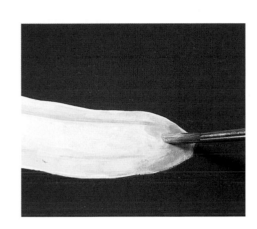

5 Use brown earth mixed with glaze, and a no.2 round brush, to paint some blemishes across the skin, and to paint the two ends of the banana.

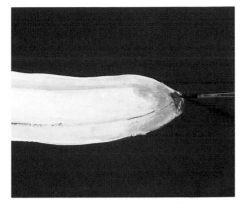

6 Shade the banana in yellow oxide mixed with glaze, using a sideloaded ¼ inch flat brush. Then highlight the fruit by drybrushing in white.

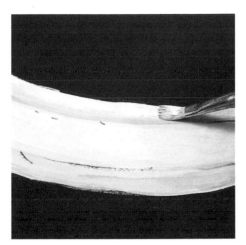

4 *Use pine green mixed with glaze, and a no.1 liner, to paint in the facets along the banana.*

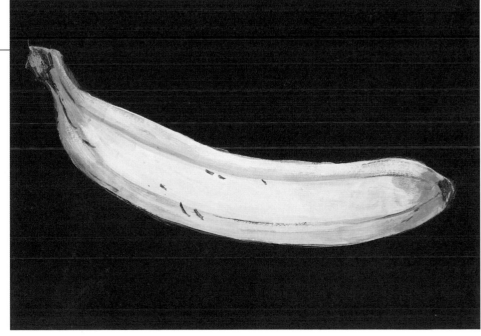

103

Inspirations

Memo and menu boards are great objects to paint using fruit, vegetable, and berry motifs because the matte black of the center panel sets off any painted color border. Other motifs can be equally as effective such as the sheaves of wheat by Hugh Logan (top right), and the chefs painted by Basia Zielinska (bottom right). For instructions on how to paint wheat see Additional Features page 121.

Memo board with fruit and wheat
Hugh Logan
The background frame of this memo board has been distressed before it was painted with a sheaf of wheat, and bands of strawberries and fruit at the top.

Ready for picking
Arlene Beck
The cool purple tones of the raspberries are subtly repeated in the pansies which make up the border of this corner shelving unit.

Menu board
Basia Zielinska
Chefs can be seen dancing in a border of vegetables that surrounds this menu board.

Oval tin planter
Katie Potter
Pea pods, carrots, tomatoes, and leeks have been painted in a random pattern around the outside of this oval planter, which gives the shapes extra movement.

PEAR

SHAPES

Cos lettuces and bell peppers,

which have gentle curves in their

middles, share the same shape as

the pear itself, although in a more

subtle way.

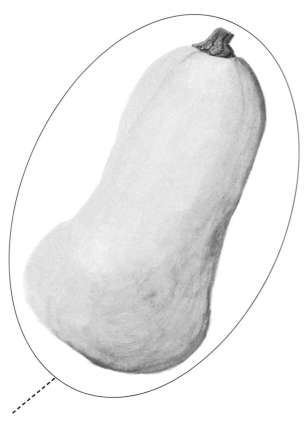

Fruits and vegetables such as the butternut squash, or the avocado that have a pear shape tend to act as anchors in a composition.

Cos lettuce

Cos lettuce has an interesting shape which can be used as the main component of a salad composition. Float layers of different green colors to give the lettuce a soft look.

Palette

1. *mint green* **2.** *sap green* **3.** *pine green* **4.** *cream* **5.** *olive green* **6.** *spring green*

Strokes/techniques

Floating color, lining

Brushes

nos.10, 1 inch and ¼ inch, no.1 liner

1 **Basecoat the lettuce in a mint green using a no.10 flat brush. Use sap green mixed with glaze and a 1 inch flat brush to tone the entire lettuce.**

2 Using a ¼ inch flat brush and pine green, shade the leaves in the background, floating the color out with glaze.

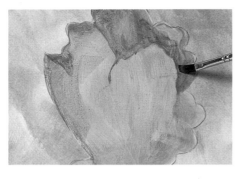

3 Outline the leaves with mint green using a no.1 liner pulling some of the green onto the leaves. Blend using a ¼ inch flat brush and float the color.

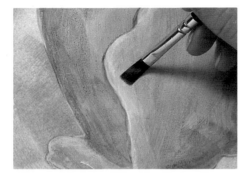

4 Use a no.1 liner and pine green mixed with glaze to paint the veins into the leaves.

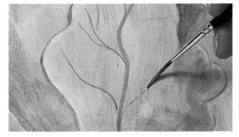

5 Paint a highlight on some of the veins, using cream and a no.1 liner.

6 Use olive green mixed with glaze to tone the bases of some of the leaves using a ¼ inch flat brush.

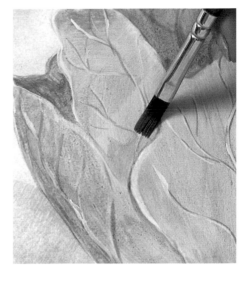

7 Brighten the lettuce with spring green mixed with glaze using a ¼ inch flat brush.

Pepper and Chilies

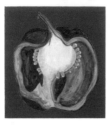

Green and yellow peppers have the same reflective depth as a tomato or eggplant, and can spice up any vegetable motif. You will find it fun and easy to paint a band or border of chilies using single strokes as described in variation 2.

Palette

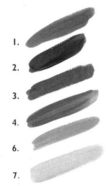

1. 2. 3. 4. 6. 7.

1. *pine green* **2.** *sap green* **3.** *olive green* **4.** *putty* **5.** *titanium white* **6.** *fawn* **7.** *mint green*

Strokes/techniques

drybrushing, lining, floating color

Brushes

nos.10, ⅛ and ¼ inch flat, nos.5 and 2 round, no.1 liner

1 Before you begin, sketch or transfer a drawing of your cut pepper onto the surface you are painting.
Basecoat the pepper in mint green using a no.10 flat brush. Paint in the deepest centers with pine green mixed with glaze using a ¼ inch flat brush. On the right side of the pepper float out the color used for shading with glaze.

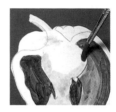

2 **Use sap green mixed with glaze and a no.5 round brush to tone the center core of the pepper.**

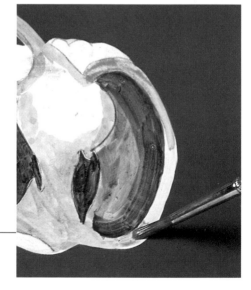

3 **Tone the cut surfaces of the pepper with putty using a no.5 round brush.**

VARIATION • 1

Whole yellow pepper

1 *Basecoat the pepper using a no.10 flat brush, and sunflower yellow. Then using a ¼ inch flat brush, base coat the stem in sap green.*

2 *Use burnt sienna mixed with glaze to shade the undulations of the pepper. Let dry. Add more layers to create more depth.*

3 *Use a no.4 round brush, and pine green to shade the stem. Highlight the stem in mint green.*

|76|80|82|84|86|88|90|94|96|98|100|102|106|108|110|112|114|

4 Use olive green mixed with glaze and a no.5 round brush to paint the outside skin. Let dry. Then with pine green mixed with glaze, shade and deepen the skin using a ¼ inch flat brush.

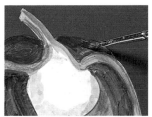

7 Use a no.1 liner and pine green mixed with glaze to outline the cut edge of the pepper. Use the liner to add some detail to the stem.

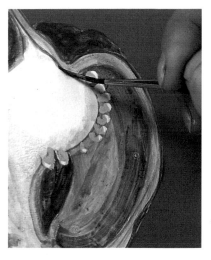

5 Drybrush the center core of the pepper with titanium white.

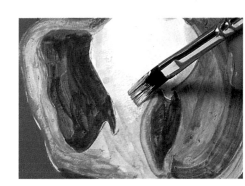

6 Use fawn and a no.2 round brush to paint the seeds. Coat twice if necessary. Add a tiny white highlight to the seeds to help them stand out against the core of the pepper.

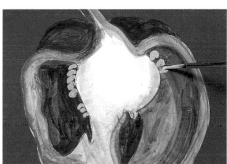

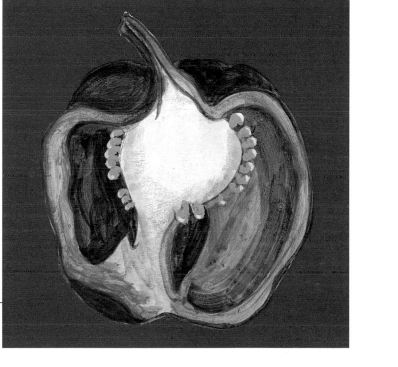

VARIATION • 2

Chilies

1 *Use a no.10 round brush with napthol crimson to make chili shapes. Begin with the tip of the brush, and pull it toward you in a slight curve, applying pressure through the stroke. Lift of to round off the shapes.*

2 *Use a no.3 round brush loaded with sap green to paint in the stems.*

3 *Using a no.3 round brush highlight the chilies in long teardrop strokes using pale pink.*

Butternut squash

Butternut squashes have a mellow-yellow color on the outside and a bright-orange color on the inside. You can include them alongside pumpkins in compositions which have a harvest theme.

Palette

1. *sunflower yellow* 2. *pine green*
3. *sap green* 4. *burnt sienna* 5. *white*

Strokes/techniques

floating color, sponging

Brushes

no.10 and ¼ inch flat, no.1 liner, nos.2 and 8 round, synthetic sponge

1 Basecoat the body of the squash in sunflower yellow, using a no.10 flat brush. Then paint the veins at the top of the squash, floating pine green with a no.1 liner.

2 Mix sap green and sunflower yellow, and float this color down the left side of the squash using a ¼ inch flat brush. Then sponge this out across the squash.

3 Mix burnt sienna and sunflower yellow with some retarder. Shade the squash down its right side and bottom.

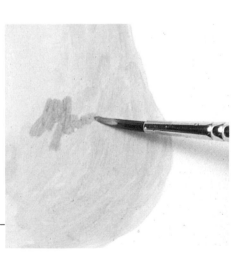

VARIATION · I

Butternut squash cut in half

1 *Basecoat the flesh in apricot yellow. Then using a no.10 flat brush, and sap green mixed with glaze, float a subtle outline around the whole shape.*

2 *Using the same brush and paint as in Step 1, paint two crescent strokes at the bottom of the squash to create the hollow where the seeds are.*

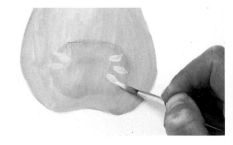

3 *Use a no.6 round brush and mint green to paint in the seeds, using single teardrop strokes.*

4 Sponge some sunflower yellow back into the squash to soften the shading.

5 Use a no.8 round brush and the shade mixture to outline the right edge of the squash.

6 Sponge a highlight onto the top of the squash using cream.

7 Basecoat the stem in sap green. Then add burnt sienna to sap green and use a no.2 round brush to paint lines on the stem. Highlight with sap green added to white.

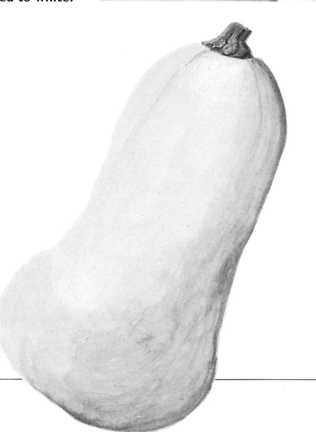

4 *Use a no.6 round brush, and sap green mixed with glaze, to paint single comma strokes on the bottom of each seed for shading.*

5 *Use burnt sienna mixed with lots of glaze so that it is transparent, to shadow some of the seeds.*

6 *Use deep orange mixed with glaze, and paint over the squash using a no.10 round brush.*

Avocado

Here you are shown how to create the texture of an avocado skin and how to paint the inner fleshy part of the fruit. You can include an avocado in any composition requiring a deep green color or a simple pear shape.

Palette

1. pine green **2.** primrose yellow
3. titanium white **4.** spring green
5. cream **6.** fawn **7.** brown earth
8. sap green

Strokes/techniques

drybrushing, lining

Brushes

nos.0, 2 and 4 round, ⅛ inch flat, no.0 liner, synthetic sponge

1 Paint the skin of the avocado using pine green and a ¼ inch flat brush.

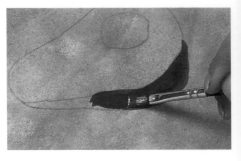

2 Use primrose yellow and a ¼ inch flat brush to paint the flesh of the avocado, outlining around the pit. Basecoat the pit in titanium white.

3 Outline the flesh of the avocado using spring green and a ⅛ inch flat brush.

VARIATION • 1

Avocado whole

1 Basecoat the avocado shape, using sap green mixed with retarder. Then use a no.10 round brush to stipple while the paint is still wet, using the tips of the brush. Let dry.

2 Stipple in the shade with a mixture of sap green and a little deep purple.

4 Use a ⅛ inch brush and cream mixed with glaze to tone the flesh.

5 Repaint the pit in fawn using a ¼ inch flat brush. Let dry. Then shade with brown earth mixed with glaze. Drybrush a white highlight on the pit.

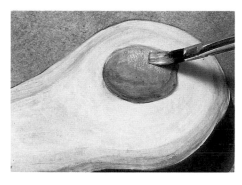

6 Use a no.1 liner and sap green to paint an outline around the avocado.

7 Use a no.1 liner and brown earth mixed with glaze to paint some lines across the flesh of the avocado. Then outline the bottom of the pit.

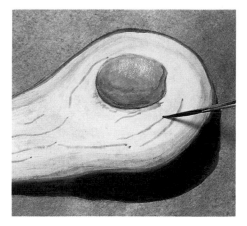

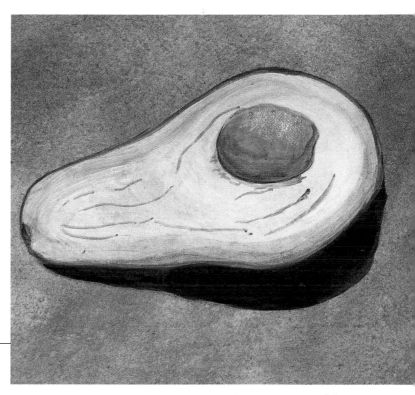

3 *Paint in the stem with burnt sienna, using a no. 3 brush.*

4 *Stipple in the highlight, using white thinned with water.*

Pear

Pears come in many colors, but here you are shown techniques for painting yellow ones. You can use the same techniques and adapt your palette to paint green pears. Yellow pears look best when they are painted on backgrounds that are deeply colored. Colors which work well are deep violets, blues, and warm browns.

Palette

1. *primrose yellow* 2. *sap green*
3. *burnt sienna* 4. *white*
5. *ultramarine blue* 6. *spring green*

Strokes/techniques

sponging

Brushes

no.10 and ⅛ inch flat, nos.0, 4 and 8 round, synthetic sponge

1 Basecoat the pear in primrose yellow using a no.10 flat brush. Recoat if necessary.

2 Using a no.4 round brush, paint in the stem with sap green.

3 Shade one side of the pear following its contours, using a no.8 round brush and burnt sienna mixed with retarder. Diffuse the paint with a sponge.

VARIATION • 1

Pear leaf

1 *Double load a no.10 flat with sap green and yellow oxide. Paint a flat scroll stroke on the upper side of the leaf.*

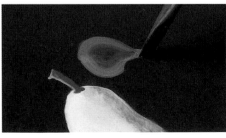

2 *Repeat Step 1 to paint the underside of the leaf.*

3 *Use a no.1 liner, and sap green, to paint in the leaf stem and some veins.*

4 Highlight the other side of the pear with white mixed with retarder, using a no.8 round brush. Diffuse the paint using a sponge.

6 Using spring green, highlight the stem using a no.0 round brush.

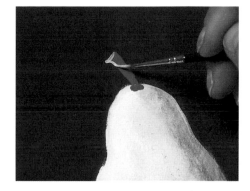

5 Deepen the shaded side of the pear using a ⅛ inch flat brush and ultarmarine blue mixed with glaze.

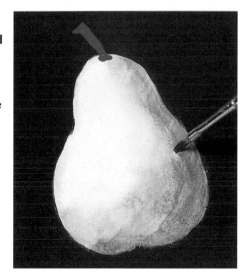

VARIATION • 2
Stylized green pear

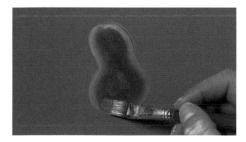

1 *Basecoat the pear using a no.10 flat brush double loaded with spring green and pine green. Outline the pear shape keeping spring green to the outside.*

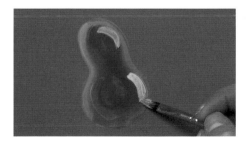

2 *Using a ¼ inch flat brush, paint two spring green comma strokes on the pear.*

3 *Use a no.4 round brush with brown earth, and paint a comma stroke stem.*

Inspirations

Sponging has been used very effectively by Marilyn Patrick-Smith to break up the background on the red bucket (page 117). You can use this technique on any object before you paint your fruit, vegetable, or berry motif. Broken color backgrounds are an easy way to add interest to a surface that might otherwise seem rather flat. For instructions on sponging see page 23.

Tin Jug
Katie Potter

This tall jug has been painted with yellow pears while pear leaves decorate the bottom. The entire piece has been antiqued to give added depth.

Fruit board
Hugh Logan

The center of this cutting board has been basecoated in black. The fruit pattern of pears, grapes, and strawberries has strong highlights which help it to stand out against the deep background.

Painted armoire
Danielle Romer

This French style armoire has been painted with an apple and pear motif which has been carried around the sides. Afterwards it was antiqued which adds another layer of depth.

116

Pear bucket
Marilyn Patrick-Smith
The red background of this bucket has been sponged to give it texture and the pear pattern has been painted over the top. The leaves of the pear have been curled to add extra interest.

Additional features

Lattice basket

A lattice-work basket is very easy to paint and can be enlarged to fit the area that you are working on by adding more criss-cross strokes in the middle. It can then be filled with any combination of fruit, vegetables, and berries to complete the design.

1 Use a ¼ inch flat brush that is double-loaded (see page 26) with yellow oxide and warm white, and paint a single continuous stroke for each band of the lattice.

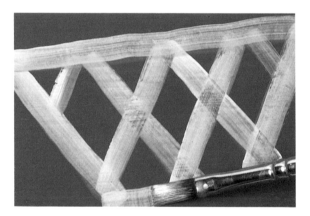

2 Paint a single connecting band across the top and bottom of the basket using a ¼ inch flat brush and yellow oxide.

3 Then using a no.4 round brush loaded with yellow oxide and tipped with warm white, paint an S stroke across the top band of the basket.

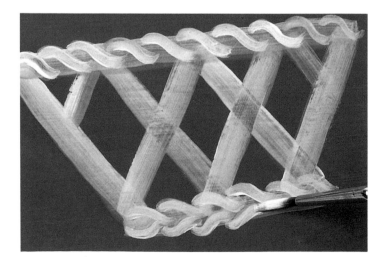

4 Finally, with a no.4 round brush loaded with yellow oxide and tipped with warm white, paint S strokes which interconnect to form a braid.

Leaf stroke border

Here a relaxed pivot and pull stroke (see page 32) has been used to create a border which gently mirrors the scalloped shape of this container. You can use this method to paint a similar border around any surface that you choose to paint. You can then add clusters of cherries, blueberries, or currants to create a simple berry design.

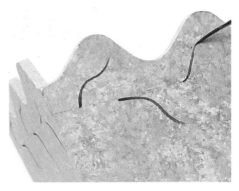

1 Use a no.1 liner and pine green to paint relaxed **S** strokes for the stems of each leaf.

2 Then with a ¼ inch flat brush double-loaded with pine green and green oxide, paint two pivot and pull strokes on each side of the stem to form each leaf.

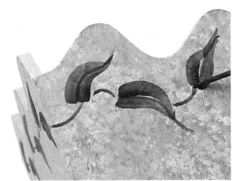

3 Paint a stem connecting each leaf using a no.4 liner and pine green.

4 Finally with a no.2 round brush and mint green, paint three comma strokes as detail on the top of each half.

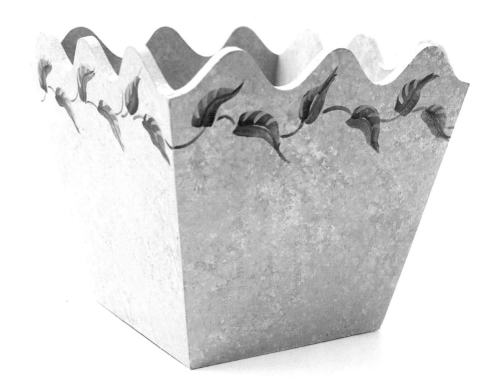

S stroke rope

You can use rope as an interesting visual device to tie together different bunches or groups of fruits or vegetables such as carrots, radishes, onions or whatever you are painting. Follow Step 1 to create a simple rope, or continue to Steps 2 and 3 to add a highlight and shadow, and to create a rope that has more dimension.

1 Use a no.4 round brush and yellow oxide to paint a simple S stroke rope band (see page 29). Allow the beginning of each stroke to connect to the tail of the preceding stroke. Be sure to give yourself a top or a bottom guide line so that you can keep your band straight.

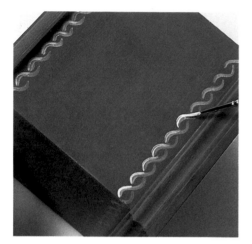

2 Use a No.2 round brush and warm white to paint a comma stroke highlight (see page 28) on the top of each S stroke of the rope.

3 Use a no.2 round brush and brown earth to paint a comma stroke shadow (see page 28) at the bottom of each S stroke.

Wheat and barley

Wheat is a flexible subject that can be used by itself as a central motif. It can be painted twisting around itself as a border and can be added to other designs. You can follow Steps 1–4 for painting wheat or you can carry on to Step 5 and paint some whiskers at the top of your wheat to create barley.

1 Use a no.4 liner and yellow oxide to paint the stems of the wheat.

2 With a no.2 round brush and yellow oxide, paint teardrop strokes (see page 29) to build up the individual grains of each stalk of wheat.

3 Paint loose formed leaves extending from the stems of wheat using a no.4 round brush and yellow oxide.

4 With a no.0 round brush and brown earth, shadow the stem, leaves, and each grain of the stalk of wheat. Your wheat is now complete. If you would like to paint barley continue with Step 5.

5 To turn your wheat into barley, add some whiskers to the top of each stalk using yellow oxide and a no.0 round brush to paint fine lines.

Inspirations

Stroke-work borders add an interesting finishing touch to objects that you are painting. Once you feel confident with comma strokes and S strokes (see page 120 for S stroke rope), you will find it easy to paint them around different surfaces as done by Dorothy Whisenhunt on the mantel clock below.

Tin jug
Lola Gill
This tin jug has several interesting elements. The apple has a water drop which gives it a focal point; the highlight on the cherries has been drybrushed, and the leaves are turning in space so that we see their backs. A couple of leaves look as if they have been eaten away.

Vegetables on wooden box
Nancy L. Genetti
The onions and scallions were painted in dark areas of color on this box, and the grain of the wood allowed to show.

Mini mantel clock
Dorothy Whisenhunt
This mantel clock has a basket which anchors the pattern of fruit that is lying along the base of the clock. A comma stroke border was used around the clock face.

Circular plate
Basia Zielinska
A combination of S strokes, comma strokes, and dotting was used to paint the decorative border surrounding this fruit pattern.

Autumn harvest (detail)
Arlene Beck
A pumpkin and a collection of ornamental squashes and gourds create the harvest theme painted on this box.

Glorious Garden Bag
Judy Shaw

A checkerboard motif outlines the pockets of this canvas garden bag which are painted with seed packets of radishes, peas, carrots, and lettuce.

Fruit tray (detail)
Basia Zielinska

The curved shapes of the slices of cantaloupe and watermelon add weight to the fruit pattern on this tray.

Grapes and daisies (detail)
Doxie Keller

These grapes are painted using a finger. Paint is applied in values; darkest first, a second value, then the lightest on top. These are "touched" up with a brush and floated color.

Painted milk churn
Clayre Sanders

Deep blue grapes and plums strongly contrast with the bright colors of the lemon, strawberries, and apples of this milk churn. A comma stroke and dotting techniques were used in the border pattern.

Glazed pears (detail)
Tirzah Probasco

These pears have been subtly blended, and together with the blueberries, have a very bright highlight which contrasts strongly to the background and helps them to stand out.

Index

Page numbers in italics refer to pictures.

A

acrylic paints 12
  thinning 22
antiquing 8, 35
apples 42–3
apricots 67
armoire 116
artichoke 76–7
aubergine 80–1
avocado 112–13

B

bag, canvas garden 124
bananas 94, 102–3
barley 121
basecoating 22
basket, lattice-work 118
Beck, Arlene:
  Autumn harvest 123
  Banquet fruit (detail) 93
  Hurricane lamp 61
  Ready for picking 104
  *Red plums and Queen
    Anne cherries* 36
beets 74–5
blackberries 64–5
blackcurrants 48–9
blending 7, 33
blueberries 50–1
borders:
  leaf stroke 119
  stroke-work 7, 122–3
boxes 61, 123
  antique tin 60
  oval 78
  wooden 92, 122

brush control 24
brush loading techniques
  7, 25–7
brushes 12
  care 14–15
  cleaning 14, 15
  double loading 7, 26
  loading 25
  sideloading 26
  tipping 7, 27, 64
  types 14
buckets 117
  wooden 78
butternut squash 110–11

C

C stroke 30–1
cabbage 52–3
candle sconce reflector 36
cantaloupe 44–5
carrot tops 99
carrots 98–9
carry-all 38
cherries 40–1
chests-of-drawers:
  harvest 79
  vegetable 39
chilies 109
chocolate-chip stroke 31
circle stroke 32
citrus fruits 88–9
clock, mini mantel 122
coffee filter box 36
color theory 16–17
color washing 23, 33
color wheel 17
colors:
  against different
    backgrounds 17
  basic 18
  classification 16–17
  complementary 17
  intensity 16
  knocking back 17

  mixing 17
palette:
  basic 18
  project 19
  primary 16
  properties 16
  secondary 16
  shades 16, 17
  tertiary 17
  tints 16, 17
  value 16, 17
comma stroke 28, 98
corn 100–1
corner shelving unit 104
cos lettuce 106–7
courgette flower 96–7
courgettes 96–7
crackle varnishing 34–5
cranberries 50–1
crescent stroke 30–1, 58
cup, tin 92
cupboards:
  country style 9
  harvest 79
currants 48–9
cutting board 116

D

dipped crescent stroke 31
double loading 7, 26
dragging 23
drybrushing 27, 90–1

E

eggplant 80–1
eliptical shapes, elongated
94–103
equipment 6, 12–13

F

Fine, Toni:
  Blackcurrants 37
  Blueberry box 78
  Cherry trug 38

  Fruit bucket 78
  Vegetable drawer piece
    39
finishing effects 34–5
flat stroke 30
flat wash 33
floating color 33
fly-spotting 35
Fortnam, Deanne:
  Blackcurrants 37

G

garden bag 124
Genetti, Nancy L.:
  Fresh vegetables 92
  Painted plaque 92
  Vegetables on antique tin
    60
  Vegetables on table leaf
    (detail) 93
  *Vegetables on wooden
    box* 122
Gill, Lola:
  Decorated miniature
    "Buckby" can 60
  Tin jug 122
glazing 33
graduated wash 33
grapes 46–7

H

heart shapes 62–77
Heron, Betty:
  Strawberry lamp 60
hurricane lamp 61

J

jugs, tin 116, 122

K

Keller, Doxie:
  Grapes and Daisies 124
  Ladies on Tray 8
kiwi 86–7

L

lamps 60
  hurricane 61
lattice work 9
  basket 118
leaf stroke border 119
lemons 88
letter-rack 37
lettuce, cos 106–7
limes 89
Logan, Hugh:
  Fruit board 116
  *Fruit bowl on
    checkerboard* 38
  *Memo board with fruit
    and wheat* 104
loganberries 65
Lowe, Kim:
  *Country flowers and
    herbs* 9
  Passion fruit wall plaque
    78

M

maize 100–1
materials 6, 12–13
memo board 104
menu board 104
milk churn 125
mushrooms 58–9

N

nectarines 66–7
negative application 23

O

onions 70–1
oranges 88–9
oval shapes 80–91

P

paint effects 23
paints 12

consistency 25
double loading 7, 26
loading on to brush 25
sideloading 26
thinning 22
tipping 7, 27, 64
palette, color:
  basic 18
  project 19
palette knives 6, 13
palettes 6, 12
Patrick-Smith, Marilyn:
  Pear bucket 117
pea pods with peas 94–5
peaches 66
pear shapes 106–15
pears 114–15
peppers 108–9
pineapple 84–5
pivot pull stroke 32
planter, tin 105
plaques 78, 92
plate, circular 123
plums 90–1
pomegranate 68–9
positive application 23
Potter, Katie:
  Oval tin planter 105
  Tin Jug 116
preparation of surfaces
  20–1
Probasco, Tirzah:
  Folk art strawberry box
    61
  Glazed pears 125
pumpkin 56–7

R

radishes 62, 72–3
raspberries 65
red cabbage 52–3
redcurrants 48–9
Romer, Danielle:
  Painted armoire 116

rope, S stroke 120
round shapes 40–59

S

S stroke 29
  rope in 120
Sanders, Clayre:
  Painted milk churn 125
  *Strawberries with flowers
    on tin* 92
scroll stroke 28
shades 16, 17
Shaw, Judy:
  Glorious Garden Bag
    124
shelving unit, corner 104
sideloading 26
sign board 78
spattering (fly-spotting) 35
sponging 23, 33, 86, 88–9
squashes, butternut
  110–11
stains 22
stamping 59
stippling 27, 90
strawberries 62–3
stroke work 7
  borders 7, 122–3
strokes, basic 28–32
surfaces: preparing 20–1

T

tables:
  drop-leaf 93
  lantern-shaped 39
  oval-topped 37
teardrop stroke 29
Thanksgiving corn 100–1
tints 16, 17
tinware: preparing 21
tipping 7, 27, 64
tomatoes 54–5
trays 8, 93

V

Vannier, Prudy I.:
  Harvest cupboard 79
varnishing 34
  crackle 34–5

W

wall plaque 78
wash mops 14
washes 23, 33
  flat 33
  graduated 33
watermelon 82–3
wheat 121
Whisenhunt, Dorothy:
  Coffee filter box 36
  Mini mantel clock 122
  Still life with fruit 39
White, Donna:
  Antiqued grapes 8
Wise, Linda:
  Fruit and flower swag 39
  *A pot pourri of fruit with
    blue birds* 37
  The yarn caddy 36
wood preparation:
  old 20–1
  stripped 21
  unfinished 21

Y

yarn caddy 36

Z

Zielanska, Basia:
  Circular plate 123
  Fruit tray 124
  Menu board 104
zucchini 96–7
zucchini flower 96–7

Credits

Quarto would like to thank the following for supplying photographs and for permission to reproduce copyright material. While every effort has been made to acknowledge copyright holders we would like to apologize should there have been any omissions.

Key: t = top b = below c = center
r = right l = left

Toni Fine 5br, 6b, 7br; Doxie Keller 3t; Kim Lowe 6t; Marilyn Patrick-Smith 2l, 11r; Tirzah Probasco 3b; Katie Potter 7bc; Prudy Vannier 2r; Basia Zielinska 4r, 7tl. All other contributing artists are credited in the captions.

All other photographs are the copyright of Quarto Publishing plc.

Quarto would also like to thank the following companies who kindly supplied material and equipment for the step-by-step photography:

Daler-Rowney (artist's materials)

Harvey Baker Design, Unit 1, Rodgers Industrial Estate, Yalberton Rd, Paignton, South Devon TD4 7PJ, Great Britain Phone: (0)1803-521515 (Blanks)

Scumble Goosie, Lewiston Mill, Brimscombe, Stroud, Gloucestershire GL6 8EJ Phone (0)1453-731305 (Blanks)

Tomas Seth and Company, Holly House, Castle Hill, Hartley, Kent DA3 7BH, Great Britain Phone (0)1474-705077 (UK supplier of Jo Sonja products)

Finally Quarto would like to thank the following:

Artwork and step-by-step demonstrations
Sandy Barnes pages 22-32, 33b, 34-35
Rachel Hammond pages 52,108, 112
Prue Lester pages 46, 64 , 68, 82, 84, 90
Sebastian Bertrand pages 1, 4, 5
Steve Tse pages 16-17
Kathie Ritchie All other step-by-step artwork

Photography
Chas Wilder

B.A.D.F. A., 1 Bentley Close, Horndean, Waterlooville, Hampshire, PO8 9HH, Great Britain (0)1705-356658